WENAMUN
ALASHIYA
RECONSIDERED

ALESSANDRA   NIBBI

ISBN O 9510704 1 X

FOREWORD

The assumption is made in introducing this study that readers are already familiar with the arguments presented in my Ancient Byblos Reconsidered (DE Publications, 1985). There I produced evidence indicating that Gebeil/Byblos was not the kbn/kpnj of the Egyptian texts (and also probably not the Gubla of the Amarna Letters). This view affects profoundly our understanding of the route of Wenamun when he set sail to get pine timber for the bark of Amun.

Further important aspects of this document are discussed here including the term Kharu or Khor, within which area Wenamun's whole journey takes place. It is important for us to define it if we can.

Apologies are offered to readers in advance for the constant re-iteration of my fifteen-year-old, fundamentally-vital theme that the ancient Egyptians never went to sea and that they did not even have a word for sea in their language. Egyptologists have now begun to accept this fact after having been unable during all this time to find a single example to prove me wrong. This is a basic factor in our interpretation of ancient Egyptian history and affects our understanding of the journey of Wenamun, as well as many other texts.

The assumption is also made here that readers are familiar with the evidence I have presented in my Ancient Egypt and Some Eastern Neighbours (Noyes Press,

1981) in which I discuss the vegetation of ancient Egypt as well as some other environmental factors which alter our choice of a location for Punt. Above all we must accept that pine, oak and even cedar in ancient times grew in areas much closer to Egypt than has been assumed until now.

The fact that we have a problem concerning Alashiya is due entirely to our misinterpretation of the story of Wenamun.

The final details in the story of Wenamun tell us that his vessel was blown off-course to IRS, vocalized Irasa/Alasa/Alashiya. A great deal of discussion has occurred with regard to identifying this country, usually accepted to be Cyprus or some part of it, but without any firm evidence. Only a few very rational scholars have been able to resist that temptation and to suggest that it must have been situated on the Near Eastern mainland.

The inland water route for Wenamun, which we suggest here, leads him to an ancient mound which is today full of sherds called El Gibali, on the south-west shore of Lake Timsah. It was still, some forty years ago, over six kilometres in extent, but has now been demolished by bulldozer.

Quite remarkably, the north shore of Lake Timsah is still today called Arasa/Arashiya, and is a part of Ismailia, the greater town that has grown up around it

comparatively recently. Clearly it was on this lake that a
fierce wind blew Wenamun's vessel northwards on to that
hostile shore. Philologists do not dispute the fact that
place-names hardly change at all over the centuries as do
words of common everyday use.

All these facts taken together are too remarkable to
dismiss or to ignore.

Alessandra Nibbi
August, 1985.

PART I

WENAMUN RECONSIDERED

PART II

ALASHIYA RECONSIDERED

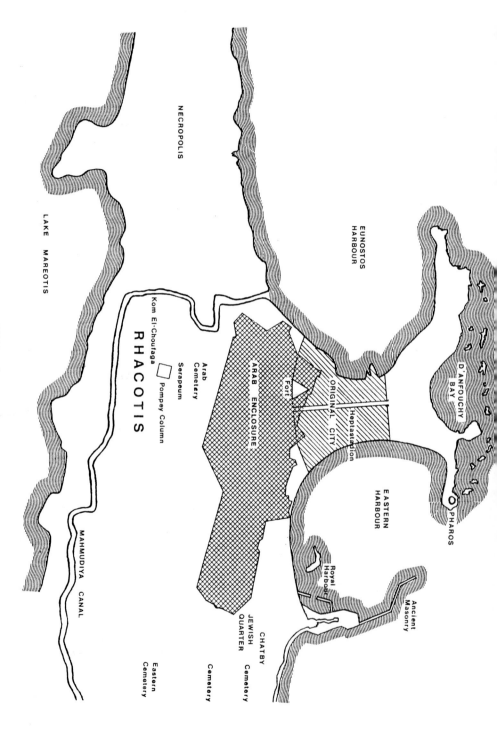

FIG. 1

WENAMUN RECONSIDERED

i) Introduction

The text of the unique papyrus of Wenamun has been used by scholars to prove all kinds of things. Among them, it is offered as proof that the ancient Egyptians went to sea, because it speaks of the great ym of Kharu upon which the ancient traveller sailed. The word for water in this context is ym, the Semitic term, which appears in the Egyptian language from the Eighteenth Dynasty onwards. However, it must be emphasized yet again that ym means no more than a water in the Egyptian context (as in Fa-yum) just as it does in the Semitic languages. Egyptologists have accepted the meaning of sea for this word mainly as the result of Golenischeff's original assumption when he first published this document in 1899, as we shall see below. Yet I have been unable to find any example where ym must mean sea from its context alone. This problem was discussed by me in a note on the Lexikon entry Meer in GM 58 (1982) and again in GM 59 (1982) as well as in other publications.

Before proceeding any further it is important to recall the Arab physician of Baghdad, Abd Allatif, writing in the fourteenth century of our own era about the salty sea. His translator Silvestre de Sacy (1810) explains to us in a note on p.7: "this expression is used by several Egyptian writers or writers on Egypt to refer simply to the sea. The reason is that in Egypt the Nile is given the name of sea, so that when they want to refer to the real sea, either the Mediterranean or the Arabian Gulf, they add the epithet salty".

In this context we must also cite the Arab writer Ibn Al-Khordadhbeh who wrote around 885 A.D.: "The Nile flows from the country of the Nuba and ends in the green Sea (al-baḥr al akhdar)" (G. Vantini, Oriental Sources Concerning Nubia, 1975). On the question of Green Sea, we have no right to assume that the Arabs or the ancient Egyptians saw the real sea as green instead of blue, as everyone else does. It is far more reasonable to suppose that the Green Sea was the area of fresh green vegetation which spread out from the narrow Nile valley into the open fan of the delta, where no borders are visible and it therefore appears to be never-ending. It is quite possible that the ancient Egyptian expression Great Green may have been the precursor of Green Sea, for the same reasons, though the vegetation at that early period was more likely to have been papyrus.

On the question of the use of the term Great Green in ptolemaic times, with reference to Rakotis, I shall not repeat here my remarks in my study of this question in GM 69 (1983), 69-80. I shall only say here that the scholars who understood these texts as affirming that Rakotis was the earlier name of Alexandria and that the old city had stood on the shore of the Great Green (-sea, sic), had not looked carefully enough at the true meaning of the geographical terminology they were using. Nor had they consulted the many maps of this city since 1400 A.D. which all show clearly that Rakotis (the area in which the so-called Pompey's Pillar had been raised) had never been included within the confines of the city of Alexandria. Only in the last hundred years or so with the extension of the city southwards has this area been considered to lie within the city precincts, but only as a foreign or "native" quarter. The reason for this is that Rakotis was situated not on the Mediterranean Sea, but on the north shore of the Lake Mareotis. It was separated from the Mediterranean Sea by a substantial limestone ridge, shown clearly on the map prepared by the Napoleonic Survey (see fig.1). It is not at all unlikely that the Egyptians should, from their earliest history, have made a distinction between the Nile proper with its two banks and the delta where the Great River divided into many streams causing swampland and a difficult terrain, quite apart from the possibility of enemy occupation of that area. The ancient Egyptian is most unlikely to have had direct access to any sea.

From the point of view of the outsider, we find Josephus (born about 37 A.D.) in his The Jewish War IV, 618, saying:

> "For Egypt is difficult to enter by land and
> the coast is almost harbourless; on the west
> it is protected by the waterless regions of
> Libya, on the south by Assuan (separating
> Egypt from Ethiopia) and the unnavigable

cataracts of the Nile, on the east by the Red
Sea, which extends as far as Coptus. Its
northern bulwarks are the district adjoining
Palestine and the Egyptian Sea, where there
is no anchorage at all. Thus Egypt is walled
in on every side ....it is difficult
even in peacetime for ships to approach the
harbour of Alexandria; the entrance is narrow
and submerged rocks make a straight course
impossible.......the sea makes the channel
rough and the entrance treacherous."

With regard to our assumption that Wenamun and others
sailed easily up and down the Near Eastern coast, sometimes
with ships loaded with heavy cargoes of logs, we should
consider the following passages, also from Josephus.
Speaking of a town along the coast called Strato's Tower,
Josephus (ibid. I, 407) says:

"The city lies midway between Dora and Joppa,
closer to Dor and hitherto the whole of the
shore had been harbourless, so that anyone
sailing along the Phoenician coast towards
Egypt had to ride the open sea when
threatened by the south-west wind; even when
this is far from strong, such huge waves are
dashed against the rocks that the back-wash
makes the sea boil up a long way out.....in
that locality the north wind is the
gentlest".

Josephus goes on to say later (ibid. III, 422):

"There is no natural harbour at Joppa, which
ends in an uneven beach straight for most of
its length but curving gently at both ends.
These are formed by lofty cliffs and reefs
running out into the sea.....Beating full on
this shore and dashing the waves high against
the opposing rocks, the north wind makes the
anchorage more dangerous than a landless sea
.........."

Even in our own day we find Karl Baedeker telling
travellers in 1898:

"Palestine and Syria are reached from Europe
either via Egypt (Alexandria or Port Said) or
via Smyrna (from Constantinople or the
Piraeus)".

Sailing into a Palestinian or Syrian harbour was
something not lightly attempted even at this late date.

It is important to take all these reports into
account when reconstructing situations and events in
pharaonic times because the winds and the seas and the
coastline were all certainly the same.

My discussion of the contents of the story of Wenamun
is as objective as I can make it and I do not begin with the
assumptions of Golenischeff, who first published the text
in 1899, with regard to the geography implied in the text.
Apart from the intrinsic implications of the text itself,
there are other considerations, which Egyptologists have
ignored so far.

Before leaving these introductory remarks, we should
recall the first detailed study of the port of Gebeil/Byblos
by Ernest Renan (Mission en Phénicie, 1864) in which he
showed clearly a coastline consisting chiefly of rocky
cliffs with a total absence of beach. Furthermore, Renan
emphasized a little bay for Gebeil/Byblos which is in fact
no more than a slight indentation in the coastline which has
been made into some kind of a harbour in the course of time
by the building of artificial breakwaters upon the existing
reefs. Renan's study showed extensive reefs along that

coast, with only two narrow channels leading to the coast at Gebeil/Byblos, one of these leading into a sheer rock face. Both channels had to be entered from a south-westerly direction which coincides with the prevailing winds and currents. But this must have made the departure of a heavily-laden vessel from Gebeil/Byblos extremely difficult because it would have had to force its way against both the prevailing winds and the currents. No scholar who has considered these facts can continue to insist that ancient Egypt imported timber from Gebeil/Byblos. My main discussion on this ancient city is contained in my <u>Ancient Byblos Reconsidered</u> (1985).

When discussing the story of Wenamun it is necessary to consider more than the identification of the towns along his route. Both his destination and the whole area within which the journey takes place must be pinpointed. The text tells us that his whole journey takes place in <u>Kharu</u> or <u>Khor</u>. Therefore this is one of the basic problems to which we must address ourselves.

ii) <u>The Main Problems Involved in the Interpretation of the Story of Wenamun</u>

The Late Egyptian story of the journey abroad of Wenamun [1] to get timber for the boat of Amun [2] is often quoted in the history books to prove all kinds of things, including the bad (sic) international relations of Egypt with her Near Eastern neighbours at that time. In presenting our facts here such a different picture will emerge that it will be fruitless to attempt to summarize all the earlier literature on this, though we hope to include it all in our references and bibliography.

The interpretation of this story until now has been firmly based on three assumptions which are no longer tenable today.

The first is that the timber which Wenamun wanted was cedar. We now know that $^c\check{s}$ does not mean cedar but probably pine.[3] We also have the indisputably-documented fact that there was a pine and oak forest in southern Palestine dating from pre-biblical times until our own.[4] There was therefore no need for Wenamun to go to the Lebanon for any timber. Even if $^c\check{s}$ had meant cedar, we can now show that the Saharan highlands have produced an abundance of cedar pollen, showing it to have grown west of the Egyptian delta probably into the early dynastic period of Egypt.[5]

The second assumption is based on the first: if $^c\check{s}$ meant cedar, then Wenamun had to go to the Lebanon to get it so that k3pwn3 must be Gebeil/Byblos. There is no evidence to link k3pwn3 to Gebeil/Byblos. It is only upon these interlocked assumptions that the place-names in this story are interpreted as indicating cities along the Near Eastern coast. This includes the lacuna in the text which is stated to be Tyre.[6]

Thirdly, the great ym of Kharu has always been
accepted as the Mediterranean Sea[7], again upon absolutely
no evidence to this effect. Kharu is generally accepted as
Syria upon the circular argument that that is where Wenamun
went to get his timber. Yet this acceptance is no more than
an act of faith on the part of scholars because Kharu as a
geographical term has never been studied in any depth. We
shall be discussing this name below. In any case, as I have
already said elsewhere,[8] to accept that any Egyptian name
refers to a national state is to accept an anachronism,
because we know that even in the comparatively late times of
Wenamun, we can speak only of city states in the Near East.[9]

As to ym, I must continue to insist that there is no
example in the Egyptian literature where it can be shown to
mean sea from its context alone.[10] It is not acceptable for
us to be told, even by an eminent scholar, simply that it
does mean sea. If there is no proof that this is its
meaning, in the form of at least one example, which is the
case also with w3d-wr, we must set this idea aside, however
inconvenient it may be to do so.

We shall not make any progress until we apply some
logic to this situation. No scholar may sensibly and
rationally continue to refer to the Mediterranean Sea in the
ancient Egyptian texts unless he can produce at least one
piece of evidence to support this. So far, none has been
forthcoming![11]

It has been said that the story of Wenamun is not
literature but a document because it is a unique record from
the pharaonic period concerning an Egyptian travelling by
water to foreign lands. Yet a great deal of mystery has
remained surrounding this tale. This is not only because we
have no comparable document or because we cannot properly
understand some of the passages. Wenamun himself tells us
remarkably little about his own intentions and purposes but
he records the reactions of others towards himself in
considerable detail. This leaves us with an unbalanced
story, raising many questions.

Much of the mystery, however, is due to our own
failure to recognize with any certainty or conviction the
places which he visited. We have also so far failed to
understand the background against which such events are to
be evaluated.

Not one of the many commentators on this story,
including the most recent one dating to 1975 [12], has seen
fit to question or discuss critically the place-names which
were nearly all irrevocably established with the first
publication of this text by Golenischeff in 1899.[13] These
were offered at that time without scientific justification,
but as suggestions which seemed to fit the story as
Golenischeff saw it. They had to satisfy the requirements
of getting cedar (sic) from the Lebanon (sic) and therefore
established Gebeil/Byblos as the goal of Wenamun's journey.

We have already discussed these points elsewhere, adding that it was unfortunate that Adolf Erman and Kurt Sethe should have adhered to these views so soon afterwards in their fundamental articles[14] that no-one consequently dared to dispute them.

The time has come not only to challenge the authenticity of our recognition of the place-names which are mentioned in the story of Wenamun but also to ask questions about the general environment against which it is to be assessed. We may well end up asking whether this traveller can have been an Egyptian at all! Yet we cannot begin by asking these questions. What we must do initially is to try to see this account firstly for its basic content, unrelated to any assumption. After that, we should try to assess its geographical and historical setting as objectively as we can.

iii) The Papyrus and its Date

The site at which any papyrus is found has its importance. In the case of the papyrus of Wenamun, Golenischeff tells us in his original publication[15] that he obtained the papyrus in fragments from two antique dealers in Cairo. He was told that in the autumn of 1891 several peasants found a clay pot containing several rolls of papyrus in the neighbourhood of the village of El Khiba. However, it is not always easy to establish the exact geographical facts surrounding an unofficial archaeological discovery, particularly in the circumstances described by Golenischeff himself, where the information was not received at first hand. One of the fragments of the Wenamun papyrus turned up in a mixed batch received by Heinrich Brugsch from Egypt. Fortunately for us all, Brugsch had been shown the original papyrus by Golenischeff and so was able to recognize the piece he had received. He made a gift of it to his colleague.

As to the date of this document, scholars seem to agree that it is to be placed in the Twenty-First Dynasty, approximately. This date is based largely on the names of the rulers mentioned in the story. But there are some inconsistencies between what we are told by Wenamun and the contents of our textbooks for this period. The ruler Nesubanebded who is mentioned in this story, usually called Smendes in the translations, is associated with Thebes (our present-day Luxor) and not Tanis in other documents from this period.[16] Yet so far, we have no record of Wenamun in the inscriptions from Thebes.

It is interesting to note that the two lines of writing on the reverse side of the papyrus of Wenamun contain names which are made up of both Egyptian and Semitic elements[17], n-ki and ns-p3-k-r-m. They refer to a commercial transaction and cannot be linked to the story of Wenamun. The hieratic writing of these two lines was judged by Georg Möller[18] to be a business hand of the Twenty-Second

Dynasty, because of its boldness.

iv) A Summary of the Basic Facts in the Story of Wenamun

The summary given below consists of the basic facts of
the story upon which most scholars agree.   Uncertain
passages are omitted and also some passages upon which
scholars do not agree.   The full original text with
scholarly annotations[19] and a number of full translations[20]
may be easily found by any reader.

In the few places in this summary where I insert a
personal interpretation of my own, which disagrees with
other scholars, I offer my explanation in a numbered note.
My subsequent comments on this story relate to its
geographical and historical aspects and are in no way
intended as a commentary on the text itself or on its
linguistic structure.   They refer to the most basic
and fundamental problems of geography in this story, which I
believe to reveal a remarkable unity in their sequence
following the route I suggest   and ending, as the story
does, with Wenamun reaching the country of Arasa, called
Alashiya by many scholars, exactly as the text says that he
does. I discuss Arasa/Arashiya as a place still called by
the same name today in Part II here.

We should preface our summary by saying that we do not
know where Wenamun began his journey. It is unlikely to have
been Thebes. He may well have set out from a city in the
Egyptian delta where there are many place-names revealing an

extensive cult of Amun,[21] the ram god.

Wenamun, Elder of the temple of Amun, sets out to obtain timber for the bark of Amun. He arrives at the river harbour of a place called ḏ^cnt [22] written with a town determinative, hereafter Djanet, where Nesubanebded and Tanetamun were. Wenamun gave them the despatches of Amun-Rē^c. Nesubanebded and Tanetamun, having read them, sent him off in a vessel whose captain was called m^cnwq3bwtj, hereafter Manuqabuty, a foreigner from the hill-country. Wenamun then went down into the great water of ḫ3rw, hereafter Kharu.

He reached a place called Djr, a foreign city[23], written with both the hill-country and the town signs. It was a harbour town of ṯ3k3rw, written with both the hill-country and town signs, hereafter Tjakaru. There the b3 of Djr, its ruler[24], had food and wine brought for Wenamun, namely fifty loaves, one jar of wine, one ox-haunch.

It happened that one man from Wenamun's vessel ran away after taking some gold and silver objects to the value of 5 deben of gold and 31 of silver. In the morning Wenamun went to the ruler of this city and told him that he had been robbed in his harbour. He demanded compensation for the money which he claimed to belong not only to him, but also to the revered gods, to Nesubanebded, to Heri-hor and to the other rulers of the Black City (written with the town sign only). Wenamun went on to say that the money was also the property of <u>B3djr</u> himself as well as of others and of <u>T3k3rb^Crw</u>, written with the Seth determinative, hereafter <u>Tjakarbaal</u>, the ruler of <u>k3pwn3</u>, hereafter <u>Kapuna</u>, written with both hill-country and town determinatives.

The ruler of <u>Djr</u> replied with expressions of respect that if the thief who had boarded Wenamun's vessel had come from the territory under his rule, he would replace the goods from his storeroom until the true thief was found. But unfortunately for Wenamun, he says, the thief belonged to Wenamun's vessel and was therefore Wenamun's own responsibility. The ruler nevertheless offers Wenamun his help in finding him. Wenamun waited nine days, then went to see the ruler, complaining that the money had not been found and that he should be on his way.

At this point the papyrus is damaged for approximately eight lines and the text does not make much sense. Wenamun passes a place called <u>D3r</u>, written with both hill-country and town signs, hereafter <u>Djar</u>.

Wenamun's next stop is with <u>Tjakarbaal</u>, the ruler of <u>Kapuna</u>. Before disembarking from his boat, Wenamun seizes 30 deben of silver, telling its owners that he would hold it against the return of his own property. He took shelter in a tent on the shore within the area of the harbour of <u>Kapuna</u> and made safe his statue of <u>Amun-of-the-Road</u> and his belongings. The ruler of the city sent him a message to leave the harbour, but Wenamun complained that he had no boat in which to travel. Wenamun asked to be sent back to the Black City (written with town sign only). But he was forced to wait there twenty-nine days while receiving daily messages telling him to leave.

Then it happened that one of the ruler's young attendants fell ill while the ruler was making offerings to the gods. He sent for Wenamun and asked him to bring the image of Amun which he had with him.

In the meantime, Wenamun had found a boat travelling to the Black City and was preparing to take the god and his belongings on board as soon as it got dark. But the harbour-master came to tell him to stay there until morning by order of the ruler. Wenamun protested that he had just found a vessel to take him home. The ruler ordered that the boat too should be delayed.

When morning came Wenamun was taken into the ruler's presence and through the window behind his back Wenamun could see the waves of the water of Kharu breaking on the shore.[25] The ruler asked how long Wenamun had been absent from his home at the Temple of Amun. Wenamun answered that he had been away five full months. The ruler then asked Wenamun where his offical papers were and he was told that they had been given to Nesubanebded and Tanetamun. Further questions followed about his vessel: where was this boat in which Nesubanebded had sent Wenamun to carry back the timber? Where was its crew originating from the hill-country of Kharu? Surely Wenamun was not going to tell him that Nesubanebded had placed him on a vessel with a hostile crew who might have murdered him and thrown his body into the water?

Wenamun protested that the vessels and crews of Nesubanebded were from the Black City and not from Kharu. The ruler then reminded him that there were twenty boats belonging to his harbour (registered? in his harbour) which were trading for Nesubanebded and affirmed that in another nearby port, there were fifty such boats plying the same trade. Wenamun could not answer this and remained silent.

The ruler then asked him why he had come and Wenamun replied that he had come to get timber for the bark of Amun in the way that had become an established tradition, carried out by the ruler's father as well as his grandfather before him. The ruler replied that his ancestors had done this only against the payment of six shiploads of goods. The ruler also expected a gift for himself. The registers of those earlier times were then produced and they found that 1,000 deben of silver of various kinds had been paid. The ruler then asked Wenamun if he thought that the lord of the Black City would have sent him gifts of silver followed by a request for a gift for Amun if it had been in his power as overlord of this city simply to demand it. The ruler emphasized that he was not the servant of Wenamun, nor the servant of Wenamun's superior.

If he, the ruler, raised his voice in an order to the master of the forests (r^cbj r nhwt)[26] the sky would open up by the cutting down of the trees and the logs would immediately be made ready for loading on the water's edge. The ruler asks Wenamun for the sails which were to propel the vessels back to the Black City and for the ropes which were to secure the logs. Wenamun is reminded of the dangers of an insecure vessel in rough waters and of the possibility that Amun might have to give way to Seth or Baal, the local god, in allowing a storm.

Though acknowledging the power of Amun and the skills of the workers of the Black Land (the land of the Black City), the ruler goes on to ask Wenamun why he was travelling without proper official backing.[27] Wenamun's answer is that no further authority is required than to be in the service of Amun. Wenamun stresses that every vessel on the river (with the canal determinative) belongs to Amun. His was the water (ym) and his, the keeper of the forest, over whom the ruler claimed absolute allegiance. To this Wenamun offered an eloquent reply.

The statue of the god Amun had been in the harbour for twenty-nine days. Was the ruler prepared to bargain with the keeper of the forest in the name of Amun? It was all very fine to say that former kings had sent silver and gold,

but if they had had power over life and health they would have
given those as gifts. Amun-Rē^c was the lord of life and
health and he was the lord of the ruler's ancestors as well
as his own. If the ruler serves Amun in the way he is being
asked, he will live, prosper and be healthy. The ruler will
benefit his whole land and his people. Wenamun asks for a
scribe to write a letter to be sent to Nesubanebded and
Tanetamun whom Amun had appointed as rulers of the north of
his land (written with the flat silt sign and grains of
sand). Wenamun offers to send for the necessary materials to
guarantee a safe journey for the timber, stipulating that
they should arrive before his departure from that city.

The messenger went off to the <u>Black City</u> in a vessel
carying seven logs[28] and returned to the land of <u>Kharu</u> in
which the city of <u>Kapuna</u> was situated, bringing four jars
and one kakmen vessel of gold, five jars of silver, ten
garments of fine cloth, ten lengths (?) of fine linen, five
hundred units of smooth material, five hundred ox-hides,
five hundred ropes, twenty sacks of lentils and five baskets
of fish.

After receiving these things, the ruler promptly set
to work three hundred men with as many oxen to fell the
trees. These were left on the ground[29] until the third month
of the summer season, when they were hauled to the water's
edge.

The ruler then tells Wenamun that he has done

everything according to the tradition of his forefathers even though he himself had not received similar benefits. Wenamun is told to load the wood and set sail without thinking about the angry state of the waters[30] because if he does so, and delays, he would see the anger of the ruler as well. The precedent is quoted of the envoys of Khaemwese of bygone days, who had been delayed for seventeen years and had died there without returning home. In order to encourage Wenamun's departure, he is asked whether he will visit their tombs, which Wenmaun declines to do. He says that he is not a rm$\underline{t}$, a mere mortal man, emphasizing no doubt his priestly status.[31]

By way of offering thanks to the ruler, Wenamun suggests the cutting of a stela and its exact wording: "Amun-Rē^C, King of the Gods, sent me, Amun-of-the-Road, his envoy, with Wenamun, his human instrument, in quest of the timber for the great and august bark of Amun-Rē^C, King of the Gods. I felled it and loaded it and supplied my ships with crews. I made it possible for them to reach the Black City and to beg for me from Amun fifty years of life over and above my given span."

Thus the stela would be there to be read by future visitors from the Black Land. The ruler thought this was a good idea. Wenamun assured the ruler that all credit for this deed would be recognised as belonging to him.

Wenamun then went to the shore where the timber lay

ready and saw eleven vessels which had come in from the lake, (ym). They belonged to the hill-country of Tjakar. Their crews said that Wenamun should be stopped and should not sail to the Black Land. At that point Wenamun broke down and wept and was taken to the ruler who was himself also moved to tears to see Wenamun in this state. The ruler ordered that Wenamun be given wine, food and a female singer to make him forget his troubles for a while. A meeting with the hostile people was arranged for the next day.

In the morning the ruler called everyone together and asked the people of the hill-country of Tjakar what it was that they wanted. They said that they wanted to intercept the vessels which were to carry their enemy to the Black City. The ruler replies that he cannot arrest an envoy of Amun in his own territory. He tells them that the only solution is to let Wenamun sail out of his harbour and therefore out of his jurisdiction, and then to pursue and arrest him, a practice which continued well into our own times in the Near Eastern Mediterranean as our next section will show.

Wenamun was accompanied on board and he sailed away from the harbour. The strong wind which was raging at that time blew the boat to the land (determinative of silt with grains of sand) of IRS, hereafter Arasa (with both hill-country and town determinatives, usually translated Alashiya[32]). The people of the town came out threatening to kill Wenamun. He forced his way through them and found the princess of the town called H3tjb3, hereafter Hatiba, whom he greets. Wenamun calls for an interpreter of the language of the Black City and one comes forward. Through him, Wenamun tells the princess that he has heard that justice is always done in the land of Arasa. He asks her whether he is going to be killed for having been blown on to this coast as the result of the storm. As for the crew supplied by the ruler of Kapuna, were they also to be killed? The princess called the people together and rebuked them for their hostility. She then invited Wenamun to rest.

At this point the papyrus breaks off and we do not know what finally happened to Wenamun. It is not impossible that he was in fact killed during his attempt to return home and that the papyrus was brought back to the Temple of Amun by some traveller as an act of piety, because Wenamun had been an elder of the Temple.

v)   The Long Tradition of Piracy, Robbery and Violence on Waterways.

The underlying elements in the story of Wenamun are piracy, robbery and some ad hoc responses by him to these situations. Such accounts are quite common in the records of travellers from any period in the world's history. They are certainly common in the ancient records of the Near East, but quite rare for Egypt, where it is mostly the official documents that have survived. This is probably why the story of Wenamun has assumed such importance in

the literature. It is the survival of the record itself
that is so remarkable and not the nature of the traveller's
experiences.

Tales similar to those of Wenamun abound in the
accounts of the early European travellers in Egypt and its
neighbouring lands during mediaeval and Renaissance times,
when piracy was not confined to the sea and its ports, but
was very common along the Nile itself, particularly between
Cairo and the two ports of Rosetta and Damietta. Some of
these later records read very much like the story of Wenamun
in the style and method of robbery and the situations in
the harbours.

Christopher Harant described in 1598[33] the typical
situation which is referred to by nearly every traveller
to these regions. During his journey from Damietta to Cairo,
Harant had the following experience:

> "After sunset, our boat was moored on the
> bank of the river, near a large town. We
> passed the night in the boat, without being
> able to move for fear of the Arabs and
> Egyptians. Because of the presence of
> robbers, it is as dangerous to spend the
> night at a mooring as it is to continue the
> journey. Often, as they are good swimmers,
> they approach the boat stealthily and while
> everyone is asleep, they climb on board,
> seize everything they can lay their hands on
> and swim off with the booty. Sometimes if
> they are successful in their first attempt,
> they come back to steal what is left. At
> other times, if they think they can seize the
> passengers, they kill them and do with their
> possessions as they wish. Travellers who want
> to maintain security on their boat buy a
> number of lighters for firing guns and during
> the night, they leave them lit all around the

boat to suggest to any distant observers that
there were the same number of guns ready. If
they happened to have a gun, they fired it as
well, as often as they could, to arouse
fear."

Another early traveller in Egypt was Johann Wild.[34]
He tells us that when his group was travelling during 1606-
1610 from Rosetta to Cairo along the river, they were woken
up by the cry that brigands were approaching. A boat was
drawing near in the darkness with only one man apparently
sitting in it. When their night guard fired upon him, about
one hundred others were seen to rise in that same boat and
to start shooting arrows at their prospective victims. But
as Wild's party had fallen asleep with their guns and
weapons readily at hand, they lost no time in defending
themselves successfully.

Vincent Stochove, who travelled in 1631,[35] speaks of
crowds of people running along the shore and swimming
alongside the boat as they journeyed on the Nile. The
passengers encouraged them by throwing them food.
However, under cover of night, the thieves among this crowd
would swim quietly to the boat, board it and seize whatever
they could. They would then immediately jump into the water
again where they could not even be seen, let alone caught.

A tale that resembles in some respects that of
Wenamun is told by Heberer von Bretten,[36] who was in Egypt
during the years 1586-1596. While he was travelling by ship
with a group of gentlemen from Constantinople to Alexandria,

one of their leather bags containing passports, jewellery,
letters of credit and money had been cut open and its
contents removed. The theft was not noticed until their
arrival at Alexandria. They went to the captain who was a
Turk and told him the facts. They asked him to do what he
could to recover their valuables, telling him that otherwise
they would have to complain to the emperor, under whose
protection they were travelling. The captain answered them
rather curtly that, had they given anything to him to be
kept safely, he would have returned it to them. But as they
had kept their valuables themselves it was their
responsibility. However, he said he would search the boat
before anyone landed to see if the thief could be found.
Nothing resulted from this. The group then reported the
matter to the Venetian consul in Alexandria, who immediately
called together some Jewish merchants of the town,
promising a reward if anyone would report any attempt to
sell stolen jewellery or to change the stolen money. In
this way the thief was soon caught and it turned out to be a
servant of the captain of the boat in which the victims had
travelled.

The early Jewish traveller Meshullam Ben R. Menahem
in 1481[37] told how the mameluke guide taking his party from
Alexandria to Rosetta, to catch a boat southwards, rose up
to slay them, creating an excuse to do so. The guide had
come armed to the teeth while the party of travellers
carried no weapons at all. They managed to survive by giving

him money. They found the camel-driver to be in league with him. There are many similar accounts of robberies on land along the roads of the Delta that were frequented by foreign travellers.

In 1591, Jan Sommer[38] recorded that between 60 and 70 robbers were operating on the Nile, between Rosetta and Cairo, but they were stealthy and not aggressive and usually the sight of a gun would scare them off. However, Sommer said that to travel on the Nile was always a dangerous thing. Because of the sometimes hostile inhabitants along the banks of the Nile, travellers could not eat, drink or sleep peacefully until the journey was over, because only rarely could the boat be stopped safely.

Jean Palerne Forésien had written in 1581[39] that these robbers and pirates along the Nile from Cairo to Damietta had been so troublesome that there was a bounty upon their heads. He himself had met two people taking robbers' heads back to the pacha to collect their reward. The robbers, it seems, took their revenge by doing the same to the travellers because Savary wrote in 1785[40]:

> "As night descends, each one prepares his arms. The Nile is full of pirates who attack boats under cover of dark, cut off the heads of passengers who are not on their guard and seize their goods".

An account which matches closely one of the situations described in the story of Wenamun is given by

Felix Fabri who was in Egypt in 1483[41]. Calling the pirates pagans, he records:

> The pagans saw a vessel on the sea on its way into port, laden with merchandise. The harbour-master of Alexandria wanted to have it captured but the Christians defended themselves to such purpose that the pagans had to return to Alexandria. We laughed about this and said that they were courageous and strong when they faced people who were defenceless but cowardly and feeble when their adversaries were armed. In the evening the same vessel managed to enter port. It was then safe, because the pagans are allowed to pillage the vessels when they are on the water but when they have entered port, they are safe."

We see from these eyewitness reports that the pirates were not always the poor farmers along the banks of the Nile, but sometimes officials in high places.

The time span embracing these accounts is a long one. It continues until the late nineteenth century when Amelia Edwards also referred to piratical activity along the Nile waterways.[42] Nothing had changed very much in the life of the local people for that half a millennium for which we have written records. It is therefore not difficult to accept that this sort of situation was common in the time of Wenamun and probably earlier as well, particularly in the waterways of the eastern delta.

Piracy and robbery are well understood by most societies today and particularly those which do not have a strong, centralized government and a highly mobile police force.

We may be surprised to learn that even on the front page of The Oxford Mail of 18th June, 1983 we find the report:

> The boss of a leading Oxfordshire boatyard is calling for tougher police action to stop attacks on river cruisers before someone is killed. His warning came after a middle-aged businessman fought off five teenage attackers who tried to board his boat as it cruised down the Thames through Oxford....He said it was up to the police to do something about the increasing number of attacks."

A traveller's difficulties along the Nile did not stem only from the presence of robbers. It could also arise from the enmity and hostility between neighbouring towns. Again we must quote from Christopher Harant (1598)[43] who described his journey from Damietta to Cairo:

> "During our journey, we saw many villages and towns without fortifications, some of them quite large, whose names were given to us. At one place, there were the towns of Serou and Rascalis, situated facing each other on opposite banks of the river. They lived in hostility and enmity from ancient times, doing all they could to cause trouble for each other."

A parallel to this situation is to be found in the story of Wenamun when he finds neighbouring towns with conflicting loyalties at no great distance from each other. Their hostilities could easily involve the innocent traveller. We are not suggesting here however that Wenamun

was an innocent traveller because he shows considerable
guile and resourcefulness in the face of his problems.

It is clear that such conditions did not apply only
to the Nile and its streams along the Egyptian delta. The
atmosphere reflected in the following passages from the
Assyrian Dictionary is very similar to that conveyed by the
account of the tribulations of Wenamun. We see from this
list that the river harbours of that period were dangerous
for a variety of reasons so that travellers along those
northern banks had to be as careful as those along the
rivers of the south. The following texts show how frequently
robbery and violence occurred along rivers in ancient times.
As we have already said, it is not the events in the story
of Wenamun that are exceptional, but only the miracle of the
conservation of this manuscript which is, in essence, a
private document.

Bearing in mind that most of the following passages
are without doubt referring to water traffic along a river
and to river harbours, we list below some phrases and
sentences from the Chicago Oriental Institute's
Assyrian Dictionary, Volume K, under kāru, meaning mooring-
place or harbour (pp. 232-239). It should be noted here that
I am resisting the temptation of suggesting that this word
is in any way to be linked with our land of Kharu even
though this is not an impossibility from the linguistic
point of view, following the rules of Von Soden's grammar.

On those pages we find:

1)...hire a boat with its crew for me in the mooring-place of Sippar....

2)...240 boats of the enemy are assembled....

3)...the enemy will take away the boats from the mooring-place....

4)...I moored five hundred small boats in the mooring-place of Diniktum....

5)...his boat was wrecked at the mooring-place....

6)...PN does not release the boats from the mooring-place of the King, they cannot continue upstream, he took over the entire mooring-place for himself....

7)...he kills anyone who docks at the mooring-place of Assyria and smashes his boat....

8)...we have been detained at the mooring-place since the 20th (of the month)....

9)...my soldiers reached the mooring-place (and) the harbour (coming) to attack them....

10)...may the mooring-place not welcome you, the embarkation point of the ferry reject you....

11)...he boarded the sailing-boat at the Holy Embankment....

12)...I blocked the embarkation point of the ferry, I blocked the mooring-place....

13)...he pays the debt to the bearer of his tablet in any harbour district (where) he is seen....

14)...the official in charge of the harbours....

15)...the gate of the harbour district....

16)...beer from the tavern in the harbour district....

17)...you must not stay (long) in the trading station in Purušhaddum....

18)...I am barred from going to the trading station....

19)...on the day when Aššur lets you arrive safely at the trading station....

20)...they must not discredit you in the trading station....

21)...he treated me like a slave, as if I had no colleague in the trading station....

22)...send out the messages in accordance with the letter from the City and make the trading stations pay the silver, let every single trading station hear the letter from the ruler and pay the silver (needed for the financing of fortifications at Assur)....

23)...a quarrel with the palace must not arise in the trading station....

24)...the trading station owed the palace 213 kutānu-garments....

25)...appeal there to the (assembly of) the trading station so that they return my tin and the textiles to me....

26)...get for me a tablet from the trading station (stating) that I have paid twenty minas of silver to his account....

27)...they (said) as follows: command of the trading station: you must not bring in (the copper)....

28)...the trading station here has held back a caravan....

29)...the watchman of the kāru has taken away (my wool)....

30)...appeal there to the trading station so that they do

not double my tax....

31)...I exempted them from (paying) taxes, harbour and ferry
dues in my country....

32)...harbour dues of the boat with the onions....

33)...from the twenty good garments which the $\underline{k\bar{a}ru}$ office
bought they returned eleven of them to me....

34)...I appointed for Egypt viceroys, governors,
lieutenants (and) customs officers....

35)...list of the officials in charge of customs stations in
fifty cities....

36)...we brought two hundred and twenty $\underline{gur}$ of dates
upstream on the PN canal but were detained in GN on account
of the customs officer, a letter of my lord should go to
the customs officer so that he allows us to pass through
the customs....

37)...the customs officer at the canal gate came aboard the
ship at night with twenty men and took (several garments, an
iron dagger and three shekels of silver) from the ship by
force....

The similarity of the events in the story of Wenamun
with the events reflected in the fragments of texts quoted
above from the Assyrian Dictionary shows that conditions of
travel, even over short distances, were difficult
everywhere. The protection that could be afforded to the
traveller was always limited by local circumstances though
the laws themselves seem to have been generally accepted.
One of the factors suggesting that Wenuman's stops were upon

inland waters seems to be the very local nature of the situation into which he usually precipitates, which is bound up with gossip and fast-travelling information, which sometimes precedes him.

vi)   Wenamun's Demand for Compensation

Among the many omissions in his story about his own circumstances and intentions during this journey is that Wenamun does not tell us how exactly he proposed to procure the timber he set out to obtain. The valuables that were stolen from his own vessel do not appear to have been of sufficient value to have been intended to be exchanged for the timber, and he appears to have nothing else to offer the ruler of Kapuna when he is actually challenged on this point later.

When our traveller goes to the ruler of Djr to tell him that he had been robbed in his harbour and to claim compensation, he guilefully explains that the treasures stolen belonged not only to himself, but to all those who had an interest in the temple of Amun. This included the ruler of Djr. But this ruler tells him, with respectful expressions, that the thief was from Wenamun's own vessel and remained therefore his own responsibility. As a courtesy, however, the ruler offers to help Wenamun to look for him.

Wenamun's demand for compensation has been discussed by Michael.Green in the context of Hammurabi Code.[44] He tells us that according to paragraph 23 of that code, a person robbed "shall set forth the particulars regarding his lost property in the presence of the god, and the town (ālum) and governor (rabianum) in whose territory and district the robbery was committed shall make good to him his lost property." Green indicates that the same procedure is attested in the texts from Ugarit, dating to the 13th century B.C. These stipulated that 1) if the offender were caught, he had to pay whatever sum was stated by the injured party to be the value of the stolen property and 2) if he were not caught, the inhabitants of the town in which the crime was committed would be collectively responsible for the payment of compensation. Green emphasizes that an escape clause was incorporated into the Ugaritic tablets namely that liability for compensation could be avoided by the citizens if their representatives swore, under oath, that the thief was not one of their number and they did not know where the stolen goods were.

Michael Green was not surprised to find that the procedures and conditions for compensation recorded in the account of Wenamun agree so closely with the Hammurabi Code and the Ugaritic tablets, because he began from the traditional assumption that Wenamun travelled to Byblos along the Mediterranean coast.

Yet this is a much more remarkable fact if we set aside that assumption, as I believe we must, and follow Wenamun along an inland water immediately adjoining Egyptian

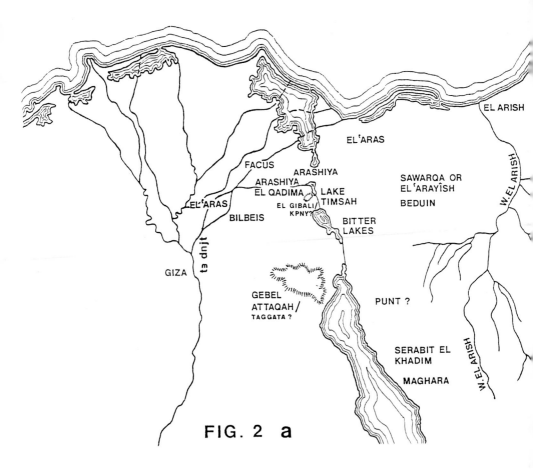

FIG. 2 a

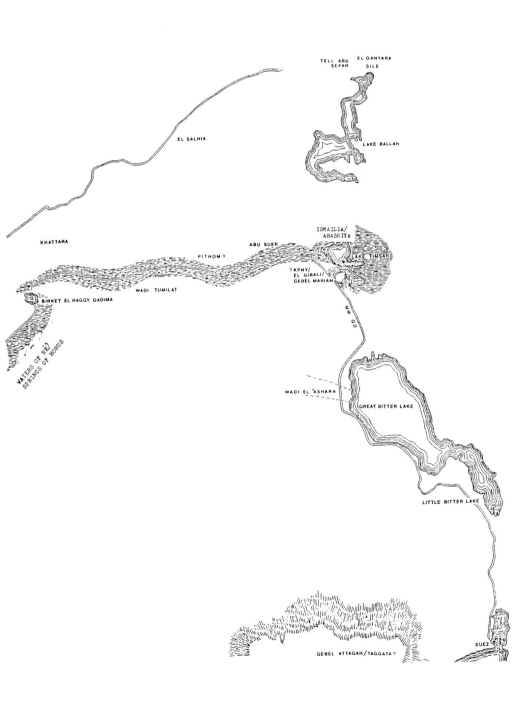

FIG. 2 b

territory and reaching no further than Lake Timsah. The only possible route for this journey is outlined in our following pages discussing Kharu, among other places, and on our sketch map fig. 8.

After nine days of waiting, Wenamun goes to the ruler of Djr to take his leave of him. It is a pity that our papyrus is damaged at this point, because it would be most interesting to know what this ruler advised Wenamun to do. We know what our traveller in fact did. He used his guile once again and seized valuables from others on his vessel as security against the return of his own property. It seems to be this act that makes him so unpopular everywhere he goes after that. We are not told how the news of his problems was so quickly propagated, but there can be no doubt that the ruler of Kapuna was well informed about his visitor before Wenamun even set foot on his territory. Otherwise his hostile reception could not be explained. This ruler, like any other ruler, did not want to encourage trouble in his own harbour.

vii) The Lands of Kharu, also called Khor

Before pursuing our geographical discussion of the story of Wenamun we must emphasize yet again that the timber that he was sent to get cannot have been cedar, but a variety of pine or fir, which was certainly available in his time in southern Palestine and the eastern delta of Egypt.[45] There was therefore no need for Wenamun to go to the

Lebanon to get his timber. This is an indisputable scientific fact. Even if he had required cedar, the text of Meri-ka-re tells us that mrw-wood, most probably cedar, was available in the west and the truth of this ancient text has been confirmed in recent years by pollen studies carried out in the Saharan highlands and elsewhere by scientists who had never heard of this ancient Egyptian text.[46]

All of Wenamun's adventures, including the final episode in Arasa (Alashiya), take place within the area which the text calls Kharu (transliterated as Khor by Alan Gardiner[47]). The usual translation from the Egyptian texts is Syria. This is another of our long-established historical assumptions which needs to be carefully examined. In no way can we accept this term to signify the political state of Syria as it exists today, nor the geographical boundaries which define it at present. During Graeco-Roman times, Syria and Phoenicia were considered to have had their southern boundaries somewhere in the northern Sinai.[48] Manetho assumed Phoenicia to begin north of Pelusium[49], see our fig.3, Judaea being considered as part of it. Pausanias I, xiv, 7 speaks of the Phoenicians who lived in Ascalon, which lies considerably to the south of Palestine. Josephus in his Jewish War (passim) speaks of Syria as denoting all the Jewish areas that we loosely call Palestine. Many references to this general area in the Egyptian Texts of the Graeco-Roman period, which we would call late texts, translate various Egyptian names as Syria and Phoenicia,

46

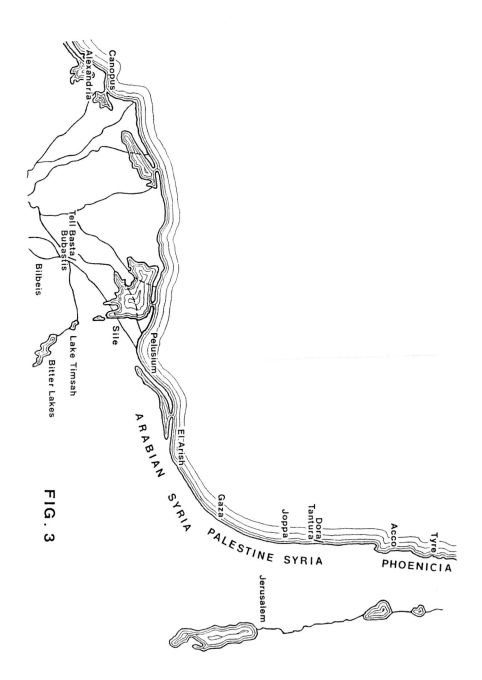

FIG. 3

which, for the earlier period, we would translate as
western Asiatic or northern hill-countries. It is not in the
translation of these terms that the problem lies, but in our
understanding of them. By using the term Syria, we
unconsciously tend to relate it to the present-day
geographical boundaries of Syria, whereas the use of this
term in the past, until quite recent times, was different.

Even in the mediaeval period the early travellers
spoke of these areas in geographical rather than political
terms. Felix Fabri in 1483 reported[50] that the Holy Land
was sometimes called Syria because both Judaea and Palestine
were part of greater Syria. Antonius Gonzales in 1665-6 told
his readers that the Nile separated Asia from Africa[51].
Richard Pococke in 1743-5 noted that Syria was made into a
kingdom under the successors of one of Alexander's
generals.[52] He also said: "Syria extends northwards from
Palestine to the mountains of Amanus and Taurus.....
Palestine indeed is looked upon by some as part of Syria."
He goes on to say: "Phoenicia was another district, part of
which was in the Holy Land and began, as some say, at the
southern part of the territory of Tyre, or as others affirm,
near Caesarea by the sea and extended northwards to the
river Eleutheros beyond Tripoli. These countries were
antiently divided into small kingdoms."

Although we accept intellectually that these Near
Eastern geographical regions consisted of city states,

sometimes united in federations of a close or loose kind, we do not apply this concept, in practice, in our interpretation of the ancient history of these areas in pharaonic times. We tend to see these regions in their present-day structure and this is revealed also by the terminology that is used in discussing the story of Wenamun. The early Egyptologists spoke anachronistically of Phoenicia and Syria and even the Lebanon. This name is thought to have been recognized in the text itself. But we must go back to using the ancient Egyptian names until we can understand better the regions they represented.[53]

It ought not to surprise us to find that the ancient Egyptians had the same concept for these regions as those that came after them. They believed that the foreign northern countries began right upon their borders and that these borders were situated approximately where the Nile ended as a river proper and became lost in the swamplands of the delta. Thus, while the Black Land is always accepted as a name for ancient Egypt, it is possible that it may be referring only to the area where the Nile silt became ammassed, namely in the delta low-lands, in the areas which were situated there in contrast to the hundreds of large mounds which were also to be found there in times gone by, up to a century ago, as Amelia Edwards found.

The textbooks which tell us that the ancient Egyptians claimed lands that were very remote from their own

Nile water, in the far north of Syria, as part of their Empire, are offering us assumptions and misinterpretations of the texts, because no proof is available for that view.

If we continue to translate the ancient Egyptian term Kharu as Syria, without qualification, as we have done since the first publication of the text of Wenamun in 1899, we are excluding from our conscious consideration the clear and important fact that emerges from the ancient texts themselves that the lands of Kharu actually adjoined Egypt and were among its closest neighbours. This fact was recognized by Wolfgang Max Müller[54] six years before the publication of the text of Wenamun, which later confirmed this. Yet this idea has not been sufficiently taken into account by Egyptologists. The best scientific approach is therefore to retain the Egyptian place-name in order not to distort the picture it presents by our own anachronistic interpretation of it.

Remarkably, the great number of written comments on the unique story of Wenamun since the 1950s never discuss the geographical names given in it. They all accept the original interpretation of Golenischeff in 1899. Even the most recent critical translation and commentary on Wenamun[55] passes on to us without comment the original geographical picture as seen by Golenischeff. No new suggestion has been offered in this respect even after Alan Gardiner studied in some detail a great number of these basic geographical terms

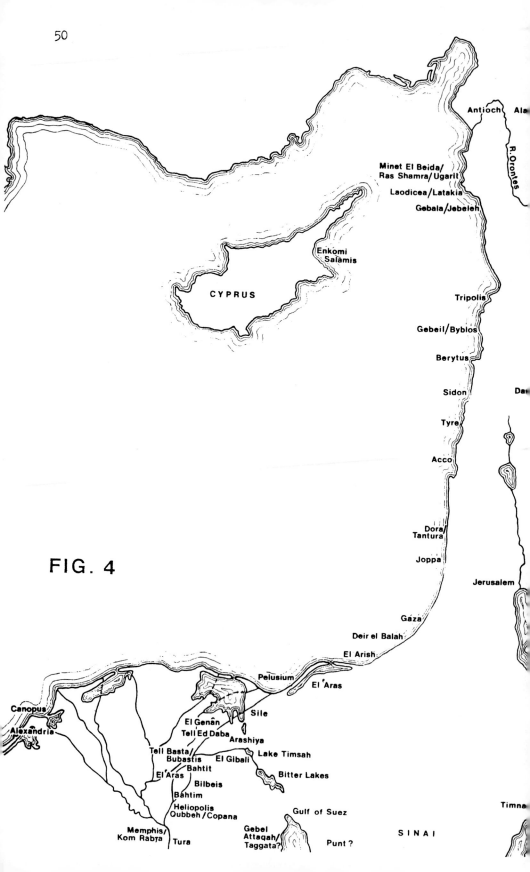

FIG. 4

in his <u>Ancient Egyptian Onomastica</u>[56]. Gardiner's discussion
followed on from the pioneering and well-documented
geographical identifications of Wolfgang Max Müller in his
<u>Asien und Europa</u> which appeared in 1893 and to which we
still refer with profit.

We owe to Golenischeff our acceptance of <u>Kharu</u> as
<u>Syria</u>, not in the Graeco-Roman sense, as beginning at
Pelusium, but in the modern sense, as a northern Near
Eastern State. This conclusion was reasonable in the light
of the limitations of our earlier knowledge: as the timber
called ᶜš was believed to be <u>cedar</u> and it was obtained from
a place called <u>k3pny</u> or <u>Kapuna</u>, which was believed to
correspond to Gebeil/Byblos, the term <u>Kharu</u> had to include
the area which we call Syria today.

However, as we have already said, recent scientific
evidence shows that every kind of wood ever used by Egypt
grew very much closer to Egypt than that. There was no need
for the ancient Egyptians to travel to the Lebanon for it.
Any chronological doubts about the existence of this timber
close to Egypt's ancient borders will not be valid because
it is an undeniable fact that a forest of Mediterranean
vegetation existed in southern Palestine from pre-biblical
times until the First World War in our own era. We have also
quoted elsewhere the evidence that pine and other
Mediterranean pollens were found at various sites of the
eastern delta of Egypt, where there can be little doubt

about the presence of fresh water and the regular deposition
of fertilizing silt in the times before the Suez Canal was
cut, because Lake Timsah was then a fresh water lake, which
also received the water drained from the neighbouring hills.
The fact that there was no lack of water and no possibility
of soil erosion in this area makes it quite certain that it
would have had an abundant and fruitful vegetation before
the Suez Canal was cut. Wenamun did not need to go any
further than these lakes to get his timber. This enables us
to set aside any speculation about how he could possibly
have brought back the long, heavy logs on dangerous sea
currents from such a distance, sailing against the strong
prevailing winds of that Near Eastern shore.

The ancient Egyptian texts make it quite clear that
when anyone left Egyptian territory, they immediately found
themselves in the land of Kharu. Max Müller was the first to
draw attention to this fact.[57] A passage from
Papyrus Anastasi III, i, lines 9-10 indicates indisputably
that the lands of Kharu began at a fortress called t3rw
situated on Nile water and that they extended northwards. A
high official is described as "king's envoy of the hill-
country of Kharu starting from t3rw to Iupa".

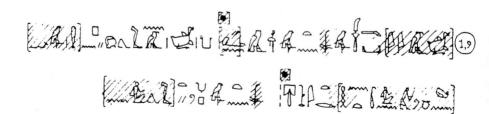

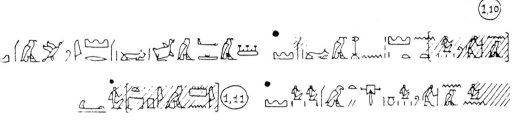

(1,10) (1,11)

after Gardiner

There is a possible implication here that <u>Iupa</u> is the northernmost limit of the hill-country of <u>Kharu</u>. If so, that limit is more likely to apply to the town of Joppa than the Babylonian <u>Ubē</u>, favoured by Gardiner.[58] Both are shown on our sketch map fig.4. But it could be neither of these.

Another passage from the earlier time of Sethos I tells us that he had defeated the Shasu people "from <u>t3rw</u> to the Canaan'.[59]

after Gardiner

viii) The Fortress of <u>t3rw</u> as the Southernmost Site of <u>Kharu</u>

The name of <u>t3rw</u> is attested from the time of Tuthmosis III and the texts tell us[60] that it was the site of a fortress in ancient times. It was accepted early as <u>Sile</u> and was equated with the town of this name in the

Antonine Itinerary and the Selle in the Notitia Dignitatum.
This was accepted by C. Küthmann and also by Gardiner[61] who
corrected the exact siting of Sile given by John Ball[62] by
telling us that it corresponded to Tell Abu Sefah, otherwise
known as Et-Tell el-Ahmar, three kilometres east of El
Kantarah (see our fig.2). In 1924 Allbright discussed the
possibility that this may have been the Zilû of the Amarna
Letters.[63]

Gardiner accepted t3rw as Sile and believed it to be
Egyptian point of departure along the so-called military
road to Palestine along the coast.[64] He accepted Sile to be
the same as the Ways of Horus, lying as it does on the
narrow isthmus between Lake Manzalah and Lake Ballah, as our
fig.2. shows. Gardiner supported his view largely by citing
the reliefs from Karnak[65] showing the Pharaoh Sethos I
marching his army eastwards. Gardiner interpreted this as
having taken place along the northern coast road, taking
into account the wells which the reliefs show as lying along
the way, though unfortunately, this part of the reliefs is
now no longer to be seen.[66] On the face of it, Gardiner
offered a rational and neat solution. But upon further
consideration, there are some objections to this view.

Firstly, we cannot yet be certain that t3rw can have
developed through satisfactorily linguistic ways into Sile.

Secondly, in my opinion, the present site of Tell Abu
Sefah for t3rw is too far north and too far east to have

afforded ancient Egypt much protection from invaders overland or by water if they came along the Wadi Tumilat, which was the most likely route to be taken by Egypt's enemies from the east in ancient times. A site much further south must be sought for ancient t3rw.

Thirdly, I do not accept that the Sethos I reliefs from Karnak represent the Pharaoh and his army marching along the northern coast road, which is the general belief at present. My reasons for this will be set out in a forthcoming study of Retenu, in which area the Pharaoh is said to be travelling in the texts. This is not merely a matter of opinion, but a necessary deduction from the general content of the references on t3rw and the manner in which these scenes are represented.

Earlier we suggested that we should seek a more southern site for the ancient t3rw. The reliefs of Sethos I show us the Egyptians returning home along a road with a series of wells and places which are named in the texts. The last two are labelled the fortress of t3rw and t3 dnjt with the determinative of a canal, translated as the dividing water and interpreted by Gardiner and others as the water at Sile which divided Egypt from the east. However, it is becoming increasingly clear that the delta was not in ancient times a wholly secure Egyptian possession and that it was inhabited largely by foreigners. If the Pharaoh and his army had reached Sile, they were by no means

56

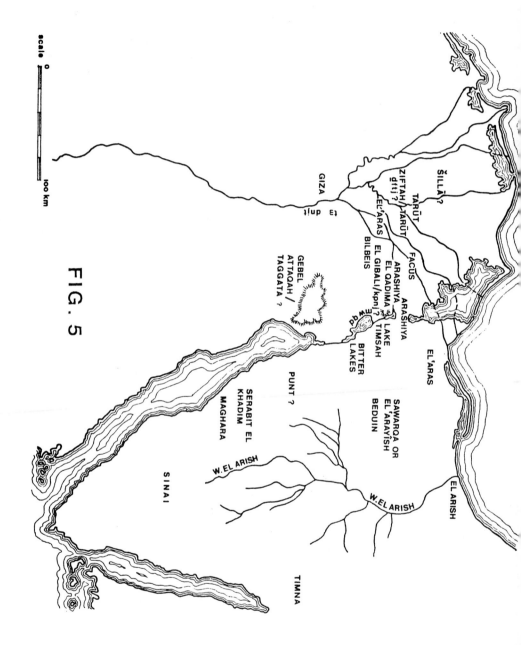

FIG. 5

at the end of their journey because there was more
hostile territory around them whichever way they were going.

There is the added point to be emphasized that
considering the enmity of many settlers in the delta to the
Egyptian ruler, it is impossible to accept that
the dividing water should refer to the water at Sile.[67] It
is much more likely to refer to the Nile river itself which
very dramatically divided itself into many streams upon
reaching the delta, thus decisively altering the landscape
and at that point terminating the possible way of life of
the dwellers along its banks further upstream. Upstream it
was possible to understand the behaviour of the Great River.
In the delta it was a totally different way for the River to
behave, and quite unpredictable. I would therefore urge that
we consider t3 dnjt to refer to the region where the Nile
broke up into many streams, because this was indisputably a
very important geographical and physical feature in the
course of the Great River, and worthy of being given a name
by the inhabitants along it (fig.2).

If this were to be accepted we should have to explain
t3rw as the penultimate port of call of the Pharaoh and his
troops on his way home to the area where the Nile was intact
as one great stream. We have two places called Tarūt which
lie in the south-eastern delta which could serve as
stopping-places along the way to the place where the Nile
water divided. For those who are irrevocably attached to

the root of Sile I would suggest also considering Šilla in
this vicinity (see our fig.5.).[68] There is no good or
scientific reason for equating t3rw with Sile. On this point
scholars have merely followed each other uncritically for
want of a better idea.

If we place the fortress site of t3rw further south
than Sile, as I believe the evidence requires, it will also
fit in much better with our interpretation of the texts
relating to Canaan and Egypt which are discussed in a
forthcoming study, though it should be said that the study
on Canaan was pursued without any reference at all to t3rw
in all its basic aspects.

It should be emphasized here that the excavations of
Austrian Institute in Cairo at Tell ed Daba (see our fig.4.)
have now revealed this to be a Canaanite site[69].
Unfortunately this site is not yet published but its
excavator has clearly indicated its character in preliminary
publications.

Tell ed Daba lies within the water of Egypt, inside
the Egyptian delta and its foreign characteristics cannot be
disputed from the archaeological finds. It is very likely
that this is only one of the many foreign settlements in
this area, attested by the many mounds which still stood in
the area one hundred years ago. These mounds which were seen
by the early explorers and visitors to the delta have been
disappearing with great rapidity in recent years because

what is destroying them is heavy mechanized equipment and not the simple hand farming implements of the villagers of the generations now passed. In most cases, these hundreds of mounds have never been studied and no-one in the past collected samples from the surface of the mounds which would have given us some information about its ancient inhabitants. This is a great loss to us all, the more so, if, as I suspect, each mound represented a foreign city and a past enemy of Egypt.

Within the framework of the evidence set out in our forthcoming special study of Canaan, this area lay along the whole northern shoreline of the Egyptian delta. According to the evidence set out there, if we accept Sile as t3rw, it would be situated within the lands of Canaan and this would contradict the content of the texts as we believe they should now be interpreted. These indicate clearly that t3rw is the southernmost site of Kharu and only just north of t3 dnjt, the land which is divided by the water as it broke up into separate streams. This would give greater meaning to the expression we quoted above from the Sethos I reliefs telling us that he had defeated the Shasu people "from t3rw to the Canaan". By implication, it would also indicate that Shasu were settled in that part of the delta of Egypt. Many will protest against such a proposal, but that is what the evidence suggests.

60

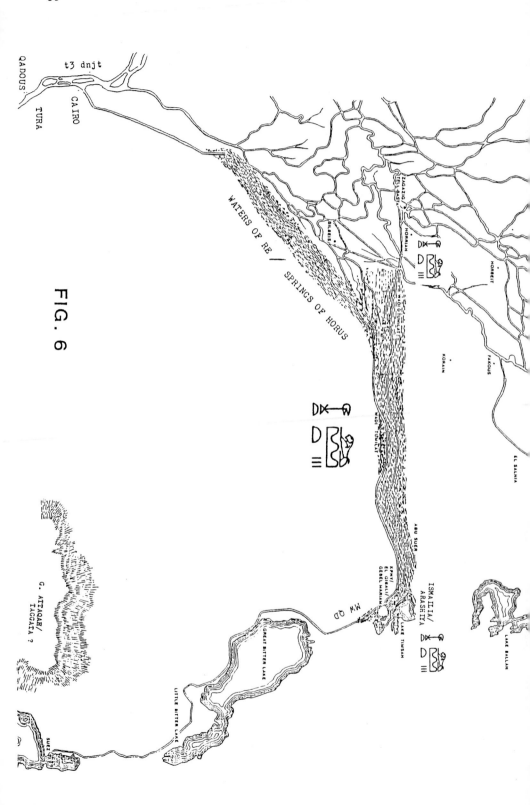

FIG. 6

ix)   The Textual Content for Kharu

To return to Kharu, Wolfgang Max Müller in 1893 quoted a number of Texts [70] which make it clear that Kharu was the first foreign region one entered after leaving Egypt proper. Egyptologists on the whole do not dispute this fact though they do not deduce anything from it, as they should. There are few difficulties in accepting the fact that Kharu began along Egypt's borders. However, it is much more difficult to establish where its northern boundaries lay, as Gardiner pointed out.[71] This is because the lands of Kharu are sometimes listed with other countries for which the present acceptance is that they are situated in the north of the Near Eastern coast: Retenu, Naharin, Ḳd, Amor, and even the Kheta countries, the latter giving rise to many problems in the Egyptian context. I shall attempt a contribution to the identification of Retenu in a later study. All these names require a detailed examination from the Egyptian textual material and cannot be included here. These toponymns must soon have a radical and substantial discussion which will be intricate because of the number of interlocked problems which they raise. It will be better to look at those terms after my initial discussion of Byblos and Alashiya in the context of Wenamun as well as the other problems analysed in my published studies so far.

I ought to say at once, however, that I do not believe that the lands of Kharu extended as far north as the state of Syria extends today. It will be enough for the present to accept the agreement of Egyptologists that the southern boundaries of the lands of Kharu began where Egypt ended, as Max Müller rightly established long before the text of Wenamun came to light.

In attempting to define Kharu, it is essential to recall its foremost product, timber. The text of Wenamun clearly tells us that he went to Kharu to obtain the valued pine (or fir) for the boat of Amun. We are told in this account that it was a tradition for timber to be obtained from Kharu by each generation for this purpose. The text itself speaks of a forest there. The journey of Wenamun is set out on our sketch map fig. 8 and we shall be discussing it in some detail later. It seems that there were some hazards in obtaining timber from this place, undoubtedly similar to those implied in the accounts of the journeys to Punt[72], though that was a much longer journey.

Apart from the presence of the abundant and fine timber, at the factual and basic level the texts give us some important clues as to the identity of the lands of Kharu by their references to the agricultural products which are most clearly delineated in the Papyrus Harris, as Max Müller was the first to note.[73] This document, which dates to the end of the reign of Ramesses III, tells us that oil, grain and cattle were imported into Egypt from Kharu, while its renowned wine is referred to in a number of other documents.

The Papyrus Harris lists on Plate 15 a, lines 4-6:

nḥḥ oil from the Black City   2743 mn jars

nḥḥ oil from the hill-country of Kharu   53 mn jars

nḥḥ oil from the hill-country of Khru (written without the
aleph) 1757 mn jars

This same document, on Plate 63c, lines 11-12 speaks of:

nḥḥ oil from the Black City, 513 mn jars

nḥḥ oil from the hill-country of Kharu, 542 mn jars.

Similarly, grain from Kharu is mentioned on Plate 53a, line 7:

grain from the hill-country of Kharu, 40 measures

and on Plate 71b, line 1:

grain of the hill-country of Kharu, 45 measures.

In this same long and informative record, on Plate 12b, line 8, we find that the lands of Kharu are written with the flat silt signs and grains of sands, as well as with the hill-country determinative. Here the text tells us that they carry an impost of nineteen bulls and other cattle.

These products suggest that the lands of Kharu must have had considerable areas of plain in order to produce grain for export and grazing for cattle, as well as food for its own population, which, to judge from the numbers of prisoners on the Mitrahina Stela of Amenophis II, seems very large. Listed separately from prisoners from Retenu and other places, the prisoners of Kharu, alone, number

36,300.[74] However, J.J. Janssen follows Elmar Edel in suggesting that these figures are exaggerated.[75] They certainly seem to be high, but this could be accounted for by the proximity of the lands of Kharu to Egypt and the possibility of survival for more of the prisoners than for more remote lands.

The production of oil in the lands of Kharu particularly suggests a southern, warm climate rather than a colder one in the northern regions of the Near East. So does its production of grapes and figs.[76]

This point is further emphasized by the fact that a number of Egyptian texts refer to the wine of Kharu, as well as to wines from other regions. It is mentioned several times in the lists of tribute in the Annals of Tuthmosis III; in the time of Merenptah, in Silsila; in papyrus Anastasi III, A, 2 (IV, 16, 1) and in the Pithom Stela of late date.[77] The suggestion is that it was a regular product of this region and a valued one. Alan Gardiner called this Syrian wine[78] and discussed these passages in considerable detail. However, no-one today speaks of Syrian wine as one to be particularly prized and I suspect it was the same in the past. Although it is possible to grow good vines in mountain regions, it is a well-known fact that they need a warm climate to grow and mature to the best advantage. It is the wines produced nearest to the Mediterranean Sea in non-mountainous regions that have always been the most desirable, because sunshine and warmth are the most important factors in their production, together with the soil itself. The recent study of two large wine presses of Byzantine date from the red soil regions of Israel[79] has shed light on the agricultural productivity of the coastal plain of Israel and also on some hitherto unexplored settlement patterns, going back to Roman times. We have only just begun to examine these regions in a scientific way.

The texts tells us that the lands of Kharu did not only consist of plains, but also had hills within their boundaries. The Karnak reliefs of Sethos I tell us that the leaders of the Shasu people had gathered together on the hills of Kharu.[80]

The earliest references to the hill-country of Kharu are from the Eighteenth Dynasty and these suggest that the area was known for some specialist craft skills. In the Annals of Tuthmosis III[81] we are told that "a great ewer in the work of Kharu" was taken as booty, indicating special and valued skills in metalwork, which bore recognizable characteristics. Such skill is also implied in a passage of the Papyrus Harris (Plate 46, lines 1-4), which includes Kharu in the area from which silver, incense and grain, as well as wine and cattle, came to Egypt. Another passage from Annals[82] mentions "five bows of Kharu" as being among the valuable plunder of a campaign. This means that perhaps

some special Mediterranean woods were used in making these
bows, though we know them to have been made successfully
with woods from a savanna vegetation.[83]

Alan Gardiner[84] noted that the lands of Kharu are
never mentioned on the topographical lists as recorded by
Simons and discussed by Jirko, though Retenu is mentioned.
Gardiner considered the possibility that the term Kharu, in
its earliest use, might not have referred to a land, but to
a people only. However, it is difficult to pursue this
discussion if we remember that both Retenu and Kharu are to
be found together on several monuments, both being used with
ethnic implications.
We find this:
a) on the list of prisoners on the Mitrahina Stela from the
time of Amenophis II[85] and on its corresponding text from
Karnak[86].
b) on the relief from the Great Temple at Abu Simbel from
the time of Ramesses II [87].

The fact that there are some examples of Retenu and
Kharu occurring together in the texts means that, originally
at any rate, some distinction existed between them in the
minds of the ancient Egyptians. We have to accept that the
lands of Kharu are as much of a political or ethnic unit as
Retenu, CApiru, Nuhasse and Shasu when they are all
presented together on a list of prisoners. Ethnic
implications for this term are certainly present from its
earliest use in the Eighteenth Dynasty, when we find two

references to a female slave named Kharjt[88] in the Kahun
papyri. It is difficult for us at present to define the
geographical boundaries of Kharu for the earlier period,
while it co-existed with Retenu in the texts, though we
shall try to do so in our forthcoming discussion of
Retenu.

By the late Ramesside period we find that the term
Kharu is being used in the late documents to the exclusion
of Retenu, to indicate the northern foreign countries in a
general sense. We have evidence of this in the Papyrus
Harris and in the story of Wenamun which is much later in
date. When we are told that Wenamun goes to the lands of
Kharu to get his ᶜš-wood, the term Retenu seems to have
disappeared from use. In earlier times, it was not Kharu but
Retenu that supplied the valued woods for Egyptian use.[89]

The range of timber associated in earlier times with
Retenu indicates a fairly extensive geographical region to
produce the conditions required for all these varieties to
flourish, from what must have been a gradually declining
Mediterranean vegetation for the ᶜš-wood, requiring moisture
and a temperate climate, to the savanna trees producing
incense and myrrh. These are stated to be essentially the
products of the land of the god, within which region Punt
was situated.[90] That the land of the god was part of Retenu
is confirmed by a number of texts which tell us that Retenu
produced copper, silver and gold, lapis lazuli and

turquoise, namely, all the precious stones of
the land of the god. The products of Retenu also included
ivory, which we may find surprising if we think of it only
as a product of the south. The evidence seems to suggest
that elephants never completely disappeared from the Nile
valley[91] in spite of the assumption that the well-known
elephant hunt at Niy took place along the river of a very
northern country. Yet it is impossible from the textual
material that we have to explain the northern boundaries of
Retenu as reaching even the southernmost boundaries of
present-day Syria. Those who persist in believing that
Retenu extended so far northwards can do so only by making
assumptions about the cities and countries mentioned in the
texts, which are said to be situated in Upper and Lower
Retenu. This problem hopefully will be discussed further in
the near future.

Kharu, as referred to in the texts of the Late
Ramesside period, including the Papyrus Harris and the story
of Wenamun, seems to be a general term for what was earlier
called Retenu. Yet these late textual references to Kharu
never seem to imply such a vast region as was the case for
the earlier term of Retenu, nor such a vast range of
products. Both Kharu and Retenu have in common references to
their $^c\underline{s}$-wood, grain, oil, wine and cattle. What we are
never told about Kharu is that it includes
the land of the god, though the Papyrus Harris, Plate 46,
lines 1-4 speaks of incense products from this region.[92] The

Papyrus Harris however distinguishes a number of times the products and tribute coming from the lands adjoining Egypt, namely, from Kharu, t3 ntr, kmt and k3š. We are never told that the precious stones of the land of god come from the lands of Kharu. Nor is ivory mentioned in this way. I have been unable to find any reference at all to Kharu in the inscriptions of the Sinai, where the general term for the western Asiatic region seems to be Retenu at all times.

In the long and important Papyrus Harris, the northern foreign countries are always referred to by Kharu, which is distinguished from t3 ntr, kmt, and k3š. We must therefore accept that these latter three regions did not form part of the lands of Kharu. The other important implication of this distinction is that kmt is treated here as a foreign land adjoining Egypt, and not part of Egypt itself.

Kharu could be approached by land. This is suggested by the Papyrus Koller I, 1-2 which says:

after Gardiner

"Apply yourself to cause to be ready the steeds of the team which is (bound) for Khor together with their stable masters as well as their grooms......" (translation Caminos[93]).

I have discussed elsewhere[94] the value of horses in ancient Egypt and the evidence which suggests that they were a royal monopoly, belonging only to members of the royal family. The very fact that such valuable possessions as horses could be sent to Kharu overland suggests that they ran no risk of suffering from the everyday hardships of the environment, as the common soldier did. Nor could the distance be so great as to wear out these valuable animals on the way.

Papyrus Sallier I, 7, 4-5 says:

after Gardiner

"When the soldier goes up to Khor there is no staff, no sandals and he cannot distinguish death from life because of lions and bears. Whilst the foe is hidden in the reed thicket and the enemy stands in readiness, the soldier goes and calls upon his god..." (translation Caminos[95]).

The reference to the reed thicket suggests an

important area of swampland, consistent with the Lake Timsah area to which we have already referred, as Wenamun's ultimate destination.

The soldier's tour of duty in <u>Kharu</u> could be as long as five years. Papyrus Bologna 1094, 9, 4-5 tells us:

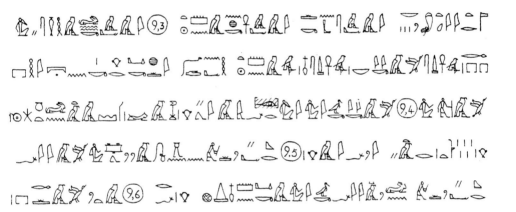

after Gardiner

"He has returned from Khor just now after five years, he having been there serving as shield bearer to Inwau..." (translation Caminos[96]).

We must not lose sight of the fact that <u>Kharu</u> was a trading area as well as a potential battleground. The Papyrus Bologna 1094, 5, 5-7 says:

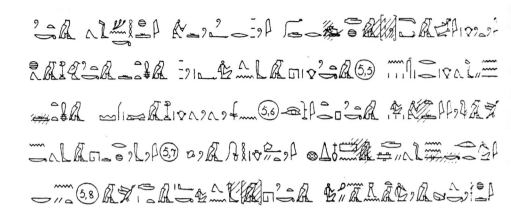

after Gardiner

"....seek out the merchant and see whether he is (yet) come from Khor" (translation Caminos[97]).

Papyrus Anastasi IV, 3:10 tells us:

after Gardiner

"Your ship is come from Khor loaded with all manner of good things" (translation Caminos[98]). Similarly, Papyrus Turin B I, 7 states:

after Gardiner

"I have caused to be brought to you through the captain of the troops of the ship Pkhore...." (translation Caminos[99]), the passage going on to tell us that various kinds of oils and horse equipment had been imported from Kharu.

The story of Wenamun as well as other texts make it clear that the lands of Kharu could be reached not only by land but by water. This does not mean that the ancient Egyptians had to go to sea to get there. It is evident from the texts that they travelled by an inland channel. Before discussing the great water of Kharu of the text of Wenamun we should look briefly at the name of Kharu itself.

x)   The Name of Kharu or Khor

It appears first in the ancient Egyptian texts of the Eighteenth Dynasty, a time when a great number of Semitic words and names entered the Egyptian language. It could well be of Semitic origin.

In his discussion of this name, Alan Gardiner rightly pointed out[100] that the problem of defining Kharu has assumed an entirely new aspect since the people called Hurrians (apparently non-Semitic in language) began to play an important part in the calculations of cuneiform scholars, because they are believed to have exerted a considerable cultural influence on the life of the Near East during the Second Millennium B.C. However, I am quite unable to discuss the Hurrians in this context. I can only ask a question of

74

those who are competent in this field: are they to be considered as the Horites of the biblical texts (Gen. 14:6; Deut. 2:12, 22), who were the early inhabitants of Seir? We can imagine that this question may remain unanswered for some time to come, for lack of enough documentation.

However, a much simpler explanation is possible for the name of Kharu and it should be attempted, though it will probably be refuted by many to begin with.

When E. Amélineau was excavating at Abydos[101] he came across a field depression called El Khor, which he went to some trouble to define. He stated that the true meaning of the Arabic word was: plain between two hills. In other words, it is the drainage passage or water-course of an area near some hills, namely, within the hills or the mounds.

We have stated elsewhere and we shall be repeating at intervals that the Wadi Tumilat was a natural drainage channel which flowed into a natural depression in an easterly direction. It inevitably carried the Nile flood downwards into the Lake Timsah area unless barriers were erected to prevent this from happening.

Our fig. 6 shows that the whole area declined into the lakes and that there were many other smaller drainage channels besides the Wadi Tumilat. There was quite a network of wadis recorded by Linant de Bellefonds in his map L'Isthme de Suez, published in 1872 but recording the area as it was in 1858.

If we were to accept Kharu as a plural form of Khor or Khar, namely a plain between two hills or a natural water-course between hills, then the network of drainage channels near to and including the Wadi Tumilat would suit this definition very well. We could then accept it to mean all that low-lying part of the Egyptian delta in the north-east which became flooded during the inundation and carried Nile water in separate channels in the direction of the lakes, even if the water did not always run the whole way along them in times of lower Niles. We recall that the Napoleonic Survey in the early 1800s noted that Lake Timsah filled with Nile water only during seasons of high inundation.

We have already said that the name of Kharu appears for the first time in the Eighteenth Dynasty which was a time of considerable foreign influence upon the Egyptian language and culture.

The Gardiner Grammar (1969[3],583) tells us that the initial sound in Kharu, namely ḫ, was in some words substituted for ḥ in later times. It seems probable that the ancient Egyptians had some difficulty in adopting a written form for foreign words beginning with the various K sounds of their foreign roots. These variations on that palatal sound are discussed in some detail by W. Von Soden in several publications[102] and it is clear that a number of these same variations occurred in the writing of these words in their <u>original</u> northern languages as well.

For this reason it would not be out of the question to associate <u>Kharu</u> with <u>kāru</u>, meaning <u>mooring-place</u> or <u>harbour</u>, as listed in the <u>Assyrian Dictionary</u>. We could think of the Wadi Tumilat as a trading area made up of almost continuous moorings all along it.

However, the fact that the name of <u>Kharu</u> usually carries the hill-country determinative and is used to designate people from there-slaves, prisoners and others - suggests that we should treat it as a more positive geographical region with some enduring characteristics. The texts imply that a person was immediately in <u>Kharu</u> upon leaving Egypt and could travel there by land or by water. It was a fertile region and thus produced food, animals and leather goods. As it was a foreign land immediately on Egypt's border, it was necessary for the Pharaoh to keep an army posted there. Horses could be sent there, valuable though they were, because the distance from Egypt was not excessive and they were certain to have their needs provided for.

If <u>Kharu</u> does in fact refer to an area of natural depression it would then end where the depression ended, namely along the lakes immediately to the east of the Egyptian delta (see maps figs, 2, 5, 6,). This certainly seems to fit the facts.

I myself have designated the Wadi Tumilat as part of the Great Green several times already[103], the other areas of the Great Green being all the swampy regions of the delta where vegetation of papyrus and other water plants proliferated. It is significant that Linant de Bellefonds showed a wide lake at the Nile end of the Wadi Tumilat near Abu Hammad, when he drew his map in 1858, before the Suez Canal was cut. It seems to have measured some four or five miles across. His map shows high ground on both sides of the Wadi, which today is totally destroyed by bull-dozer and irretrievably lost, without the possibility of finding any parallel for it in the future.

It is not impossible that the whole natural drainage system of the Wadi Tumilat, including the minor channels flowing into it may have been called Kharu in ancient times and may perhaps have implied a plural form as we see it written in the Pithom Stela of late date (Urk. II, 96). Within this area, it is possible that only the green swampland was called Great Green, as part of the total Great Green area of the delta region.

xi)   Wenamun and the Great Water of Kharu

Since the publication of this papyrus in 1899 by Golenischeff it has been accepted that the great ym of Kharu was the Mediterranean Sea simply because Wenamun went to get what was believed to be cedar from kbn/kpny which, it was believed, could refer only to Gebeil/Byblos. This picture

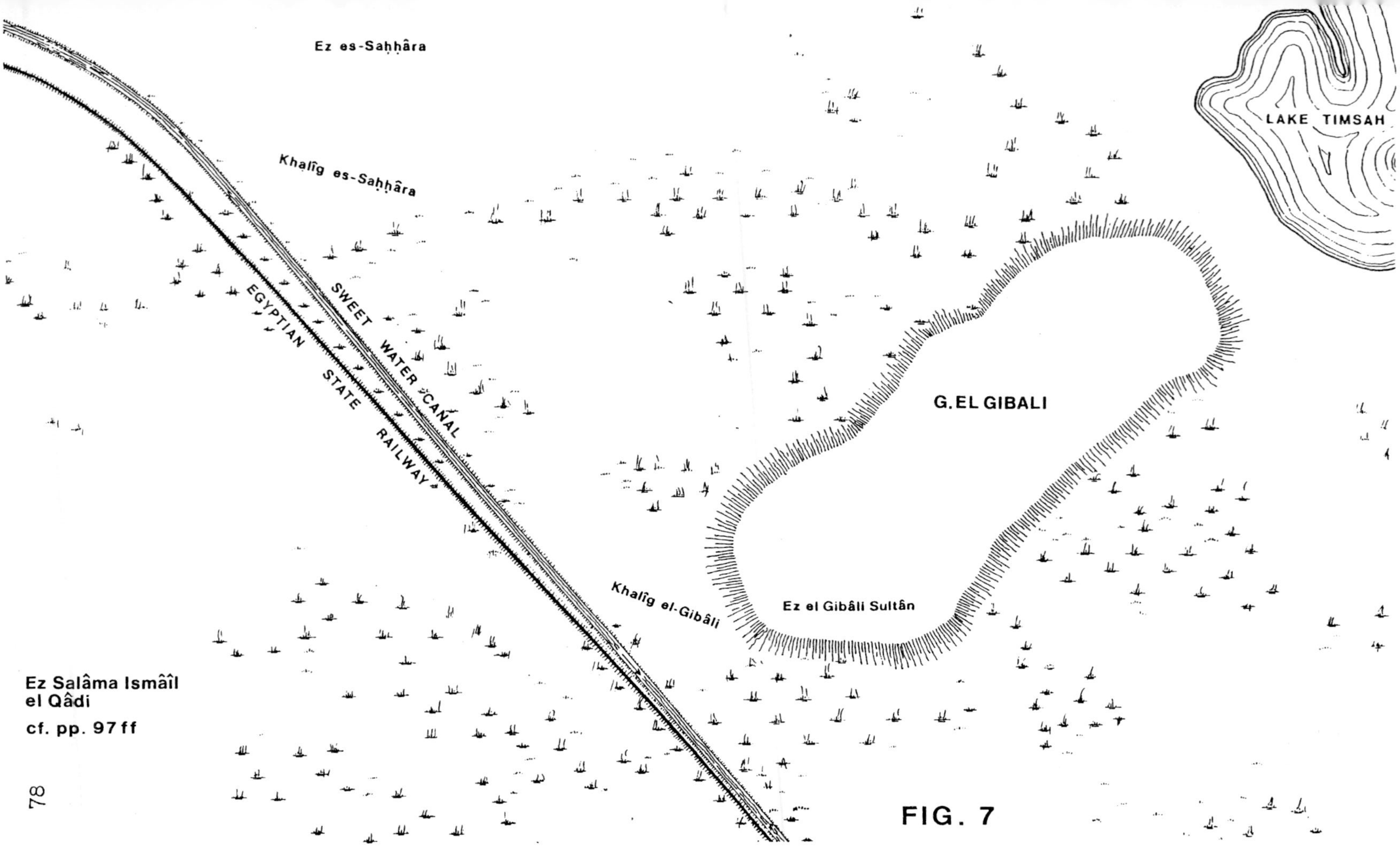

Ez Salâma Ismâîl
el Qâdi
cf. pp. 97 ff

Ez es-Sahhâra

Khalîg es-Sahhâra

EGYPTIAN STATE RAILWAY

SWEET WATER ?CANAL

Khalîg el-Gibâli

Ez el Gibâli Sultân

G. EL GIBALI

LAKE TIMSAH

FIG. 7

now needs to be corrected.

Until I began to consider in greater depth the detail of the story of Wenamun and the evidence for the forest growing very close to Egypt in ancient times, I too believed the traditional picture. However, having found no evidence at all for this interpretation after many long years' consideration of it, I now feel obliged to challenge the acceptance of ym as sea in any Egyptian context at all, as well as the acceptance of Kharu as a northern land along the Near Eastern coast. Clearly we must all accept that Kharu began where ancient Egypt had its boundaries, just north of the region where the waters of the Nile divided and in the eastern sector of the delta, as the texts indicate.

Many years have passed since I first presented my case with regard to the expression Great Green, w3d-wr, for which neither I nor my critics could find any example to mean sea[104]. This case must now be taken further. If we honestly acknowledge the fact that we do not have one, single example in the ancient Egyptian texts where ym must mean sea from its context alone, as scientific linguistic practice and common sense require, we must accept the fact that ym does not mean sea in the story of Wenamun either. The same scientific criteria must be applied to ym as to w3d-wr. We cannot say that either of these expressions means sea unless we can produce at least one example to prove this point. I have been unable to find any such example. My critics have in the past said that such examples exist, but could only quote ptolemaic texts, with an interpretation which shows no understanding of the geographical history of Alexandria. I have offered my reply to this aspect of the problem elsewhere[105].

Some responsibility for the delay in considering this problem will have to be carried by the editor of the Lexikon für Ägyptologie, Wolfgang Helck, whose entry under Meer simply reinforced the traditional assumption for the non-specialist[106]. He assumes an air of infallibility when he informs us that the ancient Egyptians used the expression Great Green to mean ocean (sic) from the Pyramid texts onwards, an idea which must have been totally foreign to the ancient Egyptians. It is certain that none of them can ever have seen an ocean and it is unlikely that many of them can ever have seen a sea!

The idea of ocean has been read into the ancient texts by scholars who did not have time to think much about the physical structure of ancient Egypt or of modern Egypt, for that matter. No-one can dispute the fact that this was in ancient times a land-locked country with no outlets to the sea, even in the north, where the many Nile streams deposited silt and left it shallow and swampy and unsuitable for navigation by heavy vessels. Today Egypt has easy access to the Mediterranean and Red Sea but even so, these hardly affect everyday life along the Nile valley proper. This is

one of the points I made in my book of 1975[107] but Wolfgang
Helck appears not to have seen it before his article on Meer
went to press in 1980, because he omits to quote it when
referring to my work. Similarly ignored have been my remarks
on the Sea Peoples so-called in the Lexikon entry
Seevölker[108].

Helck also tells us that the earlier expression for
ocean (sic) was assumed in the New Kingdom by šn-wr,
Great Circle! Moreover, he tells that in the New Kingdom,
the Semitic loan word ym comes to join Great Green in
meaning sea. He concedes, however, that ym can also mean
lake as is attested in the name of Fayum, from p3 ym. None
of these statements can be proved by Helck nor have many
attempts been made by scholars to re-examine these terms in
good faith and in the cold light of reason. Helck's article
in the Lexikon summarizes all our assumptions concerning sea
and seagoing on the part of the ancient Egyptians, including
all the absurdities implied by their acceptance, without
attempting to adhere to the scientific obligation of facing
the questions I have been raising since 1972. Egyptologists,
like scholars in other disciplines, look for guidance in
areas in which they do not specialize and they are entitled
to find such guidance in the Lexikon. But unfortunately it
is very often not there. Referring to my work Helck says
"Behauptungen, w3d-wr sei nie fur "Meer" benutzt worden,
lassen sich leicht widerlegen". Yet he makes no attempt to
do this[109]. He does not produce a single, irrefutable

example to prove his point. He merely repeats the traditional list of generalities and assumptions which only cloud the issue and which will inevitably be interpreted quite differently in the course of time, when a more literal and more objective understanding of them will have to become the accepted one.

This scholar cites the story of Wenamun as proof that ym means sea and also the story of the Shipwrecked Sailor, disbelieving, like many other Egyptologists, that the waters of the Nile could ever rage sufficiently to overturn a boat and drown its crew in spite of the abundance of historical evidence that they continued to do so into mediaeval times and later. We have already quoted some of these events and will return to them in the next section which deals with the bad weather encountered by Wenamun.

It must be conceded, however, that it is now extremely difficult to stand back from the accepted geographical picture surrounding Wenamun and to look at this document in a totally objective way. It involves reconsidering many of the most basic concepts which have become firmly established in the written history of ancient Egypt. We shall require considerable discussion on the part of serious scholars to achieve eventually a greater precision in the use of our geographical terms. But they will have to show greater courage than has been the case so far.

When we are told that Wenamun set out to get his timber by descending upon the great ym or water of Kharu, we must look for a large expanse of water leading away from the borders of Egypt which would take him into an area of forest.

We have already referred several times to the pine and oak forest which existed in southern Palestine from pre-biblical times until our own and would still be there today if it had not been cut down during the First World War[110]. We have also referred elsewhere to the pollen evidence for pine and other Mediterranean vegetation in bore samples from the delta of Egypt. This suggests that the forest of southern Palestine may once have extended as far south as this region. It is probable that in the course of time the timber nearest to the Egyptian border was used up and that it may gradually have become necessary to go further east as it became scarcer. We need more work to be done on the pollens and stratifications of this area, to give us a more accurate picture of the situation in pharaonic times.

No-one can any longer insist that Wenamun had to go to the Lebanon for his timber. Nor can we suggest that he travelled to southern Palestine by sea, because the coastline there is inhospitable, being sandy and lined with impenetrable mountains for the most part. We have already discussed these features in our introductory remarks. It is therefore certain that Wenamun travelled along the only waterway to the east from Egypt, the Wadi Tumilat. I am

84

FIG. 8

Proposed route taken by
Wenamun to kbn/kpnj/El Gibali
and then to Arashiya.

constantly referring to this route because it was the way to the Sinai and Punt in ancient times, as well as to kbn/kpny, all three lying in the same direction as the texts suggest.[111]

From the time that Wenamun leaves Egypt by descending (i.e. going downstream) upon the great water of Kharu until the time he receives his timber in Kapuna, the text makes it clear that he is always within the territory of the lands of Kharu. Wenamun's route takes him to Djanet, to Djr, a harbour town of the Tjakarw, later passing a town called Djar and arriving at Kapuna as his final destination. The fact that Kapuna is still within the lands of Kharu is confirmed in the text when his messenger's vessel returns laden with gifts.

Above all, we can now produce evidence that the coastal area of Arasa, to which Wenamun's vessel was driven by a storm, all still within the region of Kharu, is consistent with having his adventures take place around Lake Timsah. Arasa/Alashiya is discussed here in Part Two.

Apart from the fact that Lake Timsah was as far east as Wenamun could go before the Nile water turned southwards, there are many other indications that this was the end of the journey for him. We have the mound of enormous proportions south of the lake, bearing the name of El Gibali, probably our kbn/kpny or Kapuna, which we discussed in our study on Gebeil/Byblos. We also have a real

area of coastline which is today still called Arashiya,
representing the oldest part of Ismailia. Our sketch map
fig. 5. will show that the whole northern coastline of Lake
Timsah is still called Arashiya as well as some land beyond
it, even though the immediate shore of the lake has been
considerably built up in recent times. This indisputable and
scientific fact alone, more than anything else, will confirm
that we are right in placing Wenamun upon this particular
water. We have already referred to the fact that Lake Timsah
was in the past, and still is to some extent today, an area
of swampland and it is very probable that Alashiya was once
an island, situated in the middle of extensive swamps.

The place-names of Dor and Tyre which are always
mentioned in the translations of this story are mere
assumptions based on a belief that the route must have taken
him in that direction. As there is no basis for this belief,
we shall simply have to return to our more probable
direction to see whether we can draw up an itinerary from
the sound of the names today. As to the Tjakarw, it is not
impossible that this name may be related to the area which
is today called Saḫḫara (not Sakkara) which is situated
along the western shore of Lake Timsah, before reaching
El Gibali (see fig. 7. here). This would be in the right
geographical position if we could accept Saḫḫara as deriving
from Tjakarw.

Taking these facts into account, it seems very

reasonable to suggest that the great water of Kharu extended from the region near the town called Korain (the springs of Kor) where there was in antiquity a large expanse of water, which divided to flow along the many wadis into the region of the lakes. It is possible that this whole area was the great water of Kharu. It will be seen clearly on our sketch map fig. 6.

Many scholars will be displeased to see Wenamun confined to such narrow geographical limits for his journey and it may at first sight seem to make it less important. Yet this reality greatly increases its importance and makes it very much more interesting for the implications which it bears.

Michael Green has argued[112] convincingly that the cities along Wenamun's route followed the legal procedures set out in the Hammurabi Code and reported in practice in the Ugaritic tablets. Of course Green accepts the textbook view that Wenamun sailed on the Mediterranean sea. However, this does not affect the valid points he makes about the community practices of the cities along Wenamun's route and the harbour rules. The aspect of the mo'ed council had been noted already in 1945 by J. A. Wilson[113]. Thus it is clear that although the Kharu lands immediately adjoined Egyptian territory, Egyptian laws did not apply there. Although this is self-evident, we need to be reminded of it because Egyptologists tend to forget when they look at these regions on the map, that in ancient times they did not belong to the Pharaoh.

It is very likely that all the towns along the waterway of the Wadi Tumilat and around lake Timsah followed the Near Eastern tradition of independent rule as "city states", though they may well have had wider associations of an ethnic or cultural kind. We tend not to identify the "city state" system, but to think in terms of larger political units such as we have today. This has prevented us from understanding many of the problems that we are facing concerning the presence of foreigners in Egypt generally, and in the delta of Egypt in particular. The consequences of this are quite far-reaching and include the interpretation of Egyptian religion and the relative importance of the gods within it. So far, it has not been generally acknowledged that some of the towns in the delta of Egypt were essentially foreign, though Egyptians were present in them.

We should not forget that some of the most powerful city states in the ancient Near East and in the Aegean were mounds no larger than five or six acres in all. Many such mounds have been destroyed without impediment in the delta in the last thirty years. They are now being destroyed much more quickly and efficiently at the present time than they ever were in the past. It is possible that by the time this is published there will be nothing left at all of our El Gibali.

xii) The Bad Weather of the Third Month of the Summer Season
     in the Story of Wenamun

The onset of winter is sudden in Egypt, though not unexpected. Some time in October, dark stormclouds gather in the sky and burst into rain, very heavily in some areas, sometimes with the accompaniment of thunder and lightning. The temperature drops considerably almost overnight. After this change, the heat of over thirty degrees which has prevailed throughout the summer does not return. By the beginning of November, winter is well established. Yet visitors to Egypt seem never to be prepared for the severe winds which prevail during all the seasons.

It is clear from the references to the weather towards the end of the story of Wenamun that the time of year was the end of the summer. Several references to this fact include the statement by Wenamun that he had seen the birds leaving for the south[114].

We must remember that the Nile reached its fullness in the summer months and by the end of the season would still have had relatively high water in its channels. However, we should recall here briefly the legend over Lake Timsah on the map Plate 31 of the Description de l'Egypte, telling us that this lake filled with water only in times of high floods. In other words, Nile water did not go so far unless it was a good Nile year. We do not know whether this applied in ancient times and before artificial barriers were erected to control the Nile water. But if this did apply in ancient times, it would be a further reason for not delaying one's departure from a foreign country, because there could be no certainty of a good Nile the year after, and if water were lacking in the Wadi Tumilat, the vessels could not move along it to return home. It would signify an indefinite stay abroad.

The weather is discussed several times in the story of Wenamun as an important physical reality, and it is always the bad weather that is described and referred to. The detail is recorded by Wenamun that he could see the large waves breaking on the shore of the lake through the window behind the ruler of Kapuna, by whom he had been summoned. The ruler himself twice warns Wenamun about the dangers of travelling in the bad season. The first occasion is when he reminds Wenamun that he must have sails of the right weight for a vessel carrying a heavy load of logs at this time[115]. The second occasion was when he had supplied the logs and wanted Wenamun to leave his jurisdiction as quickly as possible.

The ruler is clearly and fearfully aware of the time factor with regard to the weather. Once the matter of the logs is finally settled, the ruler of Kapuna tells Wenamun that he will accept no excuses for any delay, not even the bad weather, which had apparently already begun. From the very moment of Wenamun's arrival on his shore, the ruler of Kapuna had understood that Wenamun's presence meant trouble for him, and he was fearful of the repercussions of helping this man who had made so many enemies along the waterway. He would not risk the possibility of missing this inundation to get Wenamun away, because there could be a long wait before the next possible occasion.

There are still many Egyptologists who do not accept that there were dangers in travelling on Nile water. Very few of us understand a river culture and the many aspects of an annual inundation. We shall therefore quote the following passages from only two of the many travellers who themselves experienced the frightening conditions of bad weather on the Nile.

In 1588, Samuel Kiechel[116] described the helplessness of people travelling on the Nile during times of high wind:

> "Because of the frightful heat, a violent wind often sprang up in the desert, so that we barely had enough time to bring down the sail and put it away before reaching the bank. Many boats sink in these circumstances and people drown because of the carelessness and negligence of the boatmen.

Such a description accurately fits the sudden arrival of the storm in the Story of the Shipwrecked Sailor.[117] It is interesting to note in passing that Kiechel describes the width of the Nile in Rosetta as comparable to the width of the Rhine at Cologne. It was wide enough for people to drown in if they could not swim or if the waters were agitated by a fierce wind.

Similarly, Vincent Stochove in 1631 [118] recorded the difficult conditions on the river. The current downstream could carry a boat as fast as two leagues an hour.

> "The river winds profusely on account of the great number of turns and curves, of strong currents, which we did not pass without great anxiety, as much because of the small size of our boat as because of the limited skills which we attributed to our crew......All along the banks we saw a number of towns and villages built on raised ground and all surrounded by water at that time as the Nile was at its highest point then; we did not approach these except to buy food or at night because of the wind.....During the day we endured a cruel heat owing to the fact that we were constantly exposed to the sun because our boat was so small and the wind so strong that no awning could be erected....On the third day of navigation we sighted the pyramids of Egypt even though we were nearly twelve leagues distant. They looked like mountains. This view seemed to us like our last because the wind began to blow so hard, making such waves that we often saw our little boat in danger of being swallowed up by the water. The wind kept increasing so that we found ourselves in great danger: it was impossible to land, bcause we should have had to reach the windswept bank, which would certainly have overturned our boat. We continued in this dangerous way for fully two hours, comforted to some extent by the fact that another boat was ahead of us. But this sense of comfort was soon turned to extreme terror, because at approximately half a league from the port, we saw this boat overturn and about twenty people fall into the water. Their cries for help were most horrible and pitiable, particularly as we could do nothing to help them because it was all we could manage to avoid a collision with their boat, which was still floating on the water, though upside down."

The sight of such a disaster occurring to a boat larger than their own made the travellers think that they were destined to a similar fate. They stripped and got ready to swim for safety, though there was little prospect of that in the strong current and rough water. But they did reach land safely and lived to tell the tale.

Those of us who have no experience of sailing on a river in rough weather in times of high water will see from these reports that at such times it flows very fast indeed. We must therefore accept that Wenamun could face such dangers even on an inland water.

xiii) Some remarks about the identity of Kharu as Wenamun's Destination

We must try to look at the chief references to Kharu in the texts against the evidence we have set out with relation to kbn/kpny and the events in the story of Wenamun. Clearly many scholars will be reluctant to look beyond Gardiner's very well argued geographical explanations in his Ancient Egyptian Onomastica and elsewhere, as well as the customary textbook explanation of the story of Wenamun, abounding in the most extraordinary assumptions. However, not one of us has any choice in this matter. We must examine the geographical evidence as we find it. If scholars then reject this more objective picture for Wenamun's journey, they must produce scientific reasons for doing so and not merely re-iterate the traditional prejudices.

The evidence I have presented suggests that Kharu could be understood as the region where the many Nile streams followed the general eastern depression into the lakes area of the eastern borders, as we see in fig. 5.

The name _Kharu_ seems to predominate in the later New Kingdom texts for the foreign lands to the north of Egypt, while the name of _Retenu_ tends to disappear during this period.

The accounts of the campaigns of Tuthmosis III are full of references to _Retenu_ and _Djahy_[119], where valuable merchandise was loaded on to Egyptian vessels or unloaded from them in many different harbours. It was suggested by the early Egyptologists that these harbours were Mediterranean ports. However, there is no evidence for this and unless some can be produced, we must be more realistic and accept that journeys into the northern delta in the swollen waters of the Nile were hazards enough for any traveller.

It is clear from the contexts in which _Retenu_ and _Djahy_ are used together that they must be distinguished from each other in some way. I have proposed that _Djahy_[120] may have begun at the point at which the river divided itself into many streams, though I am still uncertain as to how far north it may have extended. My proposal was that _Djahy_ should be accepted to mean _literally_ what this compound noun suggests, namely _an area where one went downstream by crossing water._ We shall be looking at _Retenu_ and its uses in due course and we shall be making some proposals for a better understanding of this name also, bearing in mind that Egyptian names are usually very closely related to the characteristics of the site or region.

Gardiner's discussion of Kharu and Khor[121] was centred strongly on the ptolemaic trilingual texts, naturally enough, because we have a better knowledge of the use of the Greek and Roman geographical terms for which the documents are more numerous.

The trilingual decree in honour Ptolemy IV[122], found near Pithom along the Wadi Tumilat (see our fig. 2) contains a passage in line 6 which is rendered in the hieroglyphic version by rd (perhaps a late writing reviving Retenu) and t3wj fnwkh, the two lands of the Fenkhu. The demotic version of this same passage is: p3 tš ꜣšr p3 tš n ḫr.w, the country of ꜣšr and the country of Kharu[123]. The Greek rendering here is unfortunately lost[124]. One thing only is clear from this passage and that is that the two lands of the Fenkhu appear to be equated with Kharu. As we shall see, this is consistent with the other data available to us. Whether Fenkhu may be related to Phoenicia is a different problem which we hope also to be considering in due course.

The hieroglyphic text of the Canopus decree[125], also a trilingual text, in line 9 says: m rtnwwt j3bt m t3 n kftt, in eastern Retenu (or in Retenu and the East) (and ?) in the land of Kftt. The Greek rendering of this text gives us Syria and Phoenicia. Thus we must conclude that the (eastern ?) Retenu was understood by the Greeks to mean Syria. In the sense of the Graeco-Roman period, this name referred to the area which began at Pelusium, approximately, and stretched northwards. I shall not comment here on the equation of kftt with Phoenicia because both of these names depend on our understanding of some others related to them, which have never been thoroughly and fundamentally discussed and therefore remain unproved. We shall be discussing Phoenicia later, but kftt will have to wait for an acknowledgment of defeat by the Establishment on w3d-wr, Great Green, before its case can be rationally argued.

Many scholars will object to my definition of Kharu by saying that if it is simply the area of the wadis which took the Nile water along the eastern depression into the eastern lakes, it is not far enough away from Egypt for Wenamun to be stranded if he could not find a vessel to take him home. The distance between the present day Zagazig and lake Timsah is approximately seventy-five kilometres as the crow flies. However, the actual distance is not as important as the nature of the settlements in this region, and the political relationship between them. Nor must we underestimate the difficulties created by the swamps in that area.

We cannot speak of this area, shown on our sketch map fig. 8 as though a journey along it by road or water were a simple matter in ancient times. We have already referred to the marauding bands of robbers in these areas both in ancient times and in our own. However, we must take into account most importantly the fact that many different groups were settled there, in an area which is relatively small but marked with a variety of strong geographical features...hills, marshland, dunes, sandy stretches and hundreds of koms or tells. We have not yet identified these foreigners precisely but we shall have to find a home there, in time, for a great many of the people shown in the rows of bound prisoners on the long lists at Karnak and elsewhere. This discussion is an attempt to prepare the ground for a better understanding of this region.

xiv) Kharu and Ḳd

Travel along the Nile channels in the delta of Egypt from ancient times until our own day, was, as we have shown, a perilous passage through a series of enemy territories, however small.

Thus when the texts associate the people of Kharu with the people of Ḳd in the records of Tuthmosis III,[126] we need not look too far afield to identify them. Rather than associate Ḳd with a northern country as scholars have attempted to do without adducing evidence for it, we should look first at regions closer to the Nile water.

Gauthier's geographical dictionary lists Ḳdj and also a town called Ḳd[127] which Gardiner believed could be a corrupt form of Kedem.[128] Nevertheless Gardiner noted that this town was also mentioned in scenes of funerary ceremonies, and not only on lists of exotic enemies.

In summarizing the general acceptance for Ḳd (Ḳdj, Ḳdw), Gardiner says that it was a region to the north of Syria, probably between Carchemish and the Mediterranean and refers us for evidence of this to Max Müller.[129] This scholar expressed his disagreement with Chabas and others before him who attempted to link this name with one of Semitic descent.[130] However, Max Müller's discussion, like Gardiner's, is based on the traditional acceptance of the names used in conjunction with Ḳd and for this reason, the discussions are misleading. Gardiner's discussion included a reminder that Ḳd is used in the Egyptian texts metaphorically in the sense of the popular English expression today: bent, meaning of bad character. This emphasizes all the more the essential meaning of this word which is related to a bend or a turn, perhaps in the geographical structure of the land to which it is related (see fig. 2.).

Some years ago I suggested that the expression mw ḳd and mw pf ḳdw referred to the Nile carried by the Wadi Tumilat to Lake Timsah, where the natural depression of the land then made it flow southwards, thus reversing completely the original direction of its flow northwards.[131] We must recognize the probability that many people lived along this fertilizing fresh water strip in ancient times and it is not impossible that they may have been known to the Egyptians by the name the Egyptians themselves gave to this particular water channel, which, completely reversing the direction of its original flow, travelled along a considerable distance before entering the Red Sea. It would be the most natural thing in the world for the ancient Egyptians to have a name for this area of their own water in Ḵdj. This is a much more likely explanation of this name than the assumption that it lay somehere in northern Syria, because of its association with other names which have also been arbitrarily assumed to lie in the far north, without any proof.

We find Kharu and Ḵd together associated with Kadesh as allies of the prince of this town[132], in the time of Tuthmosis III. The name of Kadesh immediately conjures up for us representations in relief of the famous battle, recorded in several documents, dating to the reign of Rameses II[133]. Scholars have accepted this as a clash between the Egyptians and the Hittites in the vicinity of the Orontes river in Northern Syria. The Egyptians had to pass through the valley of the ᶜš in order to get there, so it was assumed that Kadesh had to be situated to the north of the Lebanon.

My objections to these views have been stated elswhere [134] but may be emphasized here yet again as to the principal difficulties:

1) The siting of Kadesh on the Orontes is based on a number

of arbitrary identifications of placenames, including the name of the river Orontes itself. This is no more than a suggestion, unproved and tentative, as are also the other names in the lists of allies and enemies contained in these texts.

2) If $^c\breve{s}$ does mean pine, then we know that pine was plentiful both in the delta (which was full of large tells and wadis leading to the east) and in the hills leading into southern Palestine.

3) Thirdly and most importantly, we have assumed that the Kheta of the Egyptians texts are the Hittites, even though the biblical texts tell us of the presence in southern Palestine of the people of Heth. Our view of these problems is far too simple a one and will need some careful and radical re-examination.

It is a pity that the scholars who have discussed Kadesh have not examined the basic terms of reference concerning this problem because we cannot rule out the fact that the Egyptian writing of this name kds could be understood as the lake of the hill country of ḳd. In the radical re-examination of the problem in due course, we shall find that the places and the events could all have occurred much closer to the water of Egypt and perhaps right upon it. Various forms of the name of Kadesh were common in the ancient world and I have found a Qadous in the delta of Egypt which might very well have been a site for the ancient battle (fig. 2). However, the passage we quoted above in which Kharu and Ḳd are stated to be allies of the prince of Kadesh is from the Annals of Tuthmosis III and not from a report of the great battle in the time of Ramesses II, some two hundred years later.

None of the many place-names and names of peoples in these texts have ever been studied in depth, so that the translation of them is never, at any time, any more than hypothetical. This includes the concept of Lebanon[135] as the source (sic) of Egypt's timber which contributed to the idea that Kadesh had to be beyond this region as we know it today. An objective view of this evidence does not require us to insist that the placenames contained in the literatures of the northern Near East should find their exact equivalents in the literature of ancient Egypt, nor vice-versa. It is true that Egypt was in ancient times a great power and a cultural attraction for the other ancient countries around her. However, we must remember that Egypt was geographically isolated and could not easily be entered, even without military opposition. Similarly, it was not so easy for Egyptians to venture forth away from their own very particular river environment.

xv)   Kharu and k3š

The references to Kharu and k3š occurring together in the texts are usually interpreted as representing the two extremities of ancient Egypt, north and south [136]. Recently I have questioned this[137] though only at a superficial level, on the following grounds:

a) the studies on k3š so far are based on many assumptions concerning the names and peoples cited in the texts, not least the nḥsj.w, to which this group belonged;[138]

b) scholars have found a close relationship between k3š and Palestine in biblical and other texts;[139]

c) its association with w3w3t is by no means proof that it lay in the south because w3w3t too has been the subject of prejudiced assumption.[140] Montet rightly drew attention to the fact that the Achmun Stone suggested a northern location for w3w3t[141] rather than a southern one. Until this name has been studied in depth, we must emphasize that it is necessary to keep an open mind on this question.

When, in Göttinger Miszellen 59, 51-60, I suggested that Facus may have been the region of ancient k3š, I was being deliberately provocative to a great extent. Yet it is undeniable that Facus must be linked with p3 k3š. In giving further thought to this problem in the future we must bear in mind the possibility that the various ways of writing this name[142] may in fact indicate different places with similar names, a common phenomenon in Egypt and throughout the Near East. Furthermore we must not exclude the possibility of the "twinning" of towns in ancient times.

I believe we must postulate a northern site for this name if we are to understand the text reporting the appointment of an jmj-r, a superintendant of both Kharu and k3š, together.[143] It would otherwise be an impossible task for anyone to be responsible for the extreme north and extreme south of ancient Egypt at the same time.

However, the evidence requires that we also acknowledge the existence of a southern site bearing some form of this name, without necessarily going as far as Ethiopia. Why do we overlook our Qūs of today, between Coptos and Esna, in our considerations? This place is listed by Al-Idrisi, who wrote before 1170 A.D., as Kūs.[144] He tells us that one came to it going south after Asyūt and Kift and before reaching Damamil, Kamula, Burran and Esna. He goes on to tell us:

> "Kūs is a large place situated on the eastern bank and seven miles from the Nile. It is a town with a large population, renowned for its commercial activity, the (bad) quality of its climate and the fertility of its soil. Its inhabitants have a yellow skin and any foreigners who come to live here become prone to many illnesses."

Clearly there were no negroes in Kūs in Al-Idrisi's day. He describes the yellow skin of the natives of this town, perhaps as sufferers of a chronic condition of poor health. However, it is also interesting to note that he refers to the foreigners who went to live there, suggesting a strong closed community in the town.

It is certain we have been wrong in translating negroes for the people of k3š, if they came from Kūs, just as much as they would have been the case if they had come from Facus.[145] The problem of k3š in all its aspects requires a profound and objective further examination.

xvi) A Summary of our Remarks on Wenamun's Route

We have suggested that the lands of Kharu may very well have been the easterly natural drainage system of the delta in which the water followed the channels between the hundreds of mounds, known to have existed there, into the area of Lake Timsah, which, until very recently was an extensive swampland (see our figs. 2 and 6).

The text of Wenamun tells us that his whole journey took place within the lands of Kharu. He sets out upon the great water of Kharu in order to sail to his destination of kapuna. The text tells us in lines II, 35-40 that kapuna too was within the area of the lands of Kharu.

We are told that when Wenamun set out from an unnamed place for the purpose of obtaining timber, probably pine, for the bark of Amun, his first stop was at a town called d^cnt. Egyptologists have until now accepted this as Tanis and I believe this to be possible because in Tanis we are still on the water of Egypt, though well away from the Great River as such and therefore from the more secure authority of the Pharaoh.

From there, within the month, Wenamun reached the town called Djr, written with both the foreign hill-country and the town determinatives. This is the place which was identified by Golenischeff as the biblical <u>Dor</u> (<u>Tanturah</u>), on the Mediterranean coast (see our fig.4). In this identification Golenischeff did not follow any particular piece of evidence, but merely assumed that if Wenamun was going to Gebeil/Byblos (sic) and travelling on the Mediterranean Sea (sic), this was a very likely stopping-place which fitted the sound of that name. This would have been acceptable as a working hypothesis, but it soon became a fixed and unquestioned acceptance, with misleading results, which overreached the boundaries of Egyptology. Remarkably, biblical scholars prove the identity of <u>Dor</u> (<u>Tanturah</u>) by quoting the journey of Wenamun on his way to Gebeil/Byblos (sic), even though this identification of the biblical city raised some legitimate doubts even as far back as 1924[146]. There is no certainty that <u>Tanturah</u> was the biblical city of <u>Dor</u> and that this city should be placed on our biblical maps in this position.

We are told that <u>Djr</u> was a harbour town of the <u>Tjakar(w)</u> and it was there that Wenamun was robbed. If our suggestion of an inland water for Wenamun's journey is acceptable, we may find it possible to associate the name of <u>Tjakar(w)</u> with the district of <u>Saḥḥara</u> (not <u>Saqqara</u>) in the vicinity of Lake Timsah, which is marked on all detailed Survey of Egypt maps, see our fig. 7 here. Philologically, this association may be made if we follow Von Soden's rules in his <u>Grammar</u>, bearing in mind that this was territory foreign to Egypt. However, in suggesting this we are doing what Golenischeff did, namely drawing attention to a similarity of names along a route which we believe to be the right one.

After a delay of nine days in D̲j̲r in an attempt to find out who stole his money, Wenamun leaves the town and the next place mentioned in the text is D̲j̲ar, which has commonly been accepted as Tyre, again only on the basis of what it ought to be on a journey from Egypt to Gebeil/Byblos (sic) on the Mediterranean Sea (sic). If I am right in suggesting that Wenamun was travelling on an inland water, then D̲j̲ar cannot possibly be Tyre and must be identified as a town along an inland waterway.

In order not to complicate my proposals here which are of a general nature, but fundamental, and for which I believe there is more satisfactory evidence than for the assumptions proposed tentatively by Golenischeff but accepted firmly since then uncritically, I am not outlining here a specific and detailed route for Wenamun's journey, because such detail at this stage must be speculative. I hope to do this later.

My purpose here and now is to show that the general aspects of the journey of Wenamun bear all the signs of an inland route, and none whatever for a sea route which would have been impossible in practice.

The final and most important piece of evidence is

that on the last lap of his recorded journey, Wenamun is swept to Irasa/Alashiya <u>on that same water</u>. We can show this to be true if he travelled on the Great Water of the Channels of the Eastern Delta leading into the swampland of Lake Timsah to El Gibali/kpnj. It is a geographically scientific fact that the north shore of Lake Timsah is still today called <u>Arasha/Arashiya</u>. We know the <u>r</u> and the <u>l</u> were interchangeable.

Let those scholars who wish to cling blindly to their past assumptions <u>not</u> suggest that in the tradition of the Near East, Arasa/Arashiya was one of the many names repeated for different cities throughout the area, like Gebal, unless they can produce at least <u>one</u> other example. I have been unable to find another, though I have looked for it.

The Arasa/Arashiya which I have found is very real, very extensive as a region and most interesting in its unexpected geographical position because it affects profoundly our interpretation of many problems, including Egypt's relations with the Hittites.

xvii) <u>Conclusion</u>

As we have seen, there are many problems involved in understanding the tale of Wenamun, which is certainly the best-known document from ancient Egypt. An understanding of this story is dependent upon considering it in its accurate geographical and historical setting. This has not been done until now. The geographical background which I propose here is based strictly on the evidence available to us so far, and I believe this enables us to accept the detail in this account much more logically than before. The detaining of a messenger for a period of years was not such a rare thing in ancient times, as we see in Amarna Letter 35, line 36.

The main points I have made in this analysis are as follows:

1) The description of Wenamun's journey as having taken place along the ports of the Mediterranean Sea was suggested by Golenischeff at the time he first published this text in 1899. They were no more than suggestions in order to enable us to piece together this story into an intelligible whole. However the identification and the acceptance of Wenamun's ports of call until now have been arbitrary and not justifiable from the evidence.

2) The evidence now shows that timber was plentiful in the delta and in southern Palestine during the pharaonic period so that Wenamun most certainly did not need to go any further to procure it.

3) There is no evidence for any Egyptian having set out on a sea journey and the very word for sea is absent from the ancient Egyptian texts. Scholars who insist that Great Green and ym mean sea, according to the traditional acceptance of these terms until now, must produce at least one example for each showing this to be the case without the need for explanation to the reader. So far, none has been

forthcoming.

4) If the Egyptian word kbn/kpny was in fact derived from the Semitic root Gbl, any mountain or hill would fill this requirement as Wenamun's destination. Following our full discussion of this in my Ancient Byblos Reconsidered we suggested that Wenamun travelled along the waterway leading to Lake Timsah, arriving at El Gibali, an enormous mound of which a small fraction still stands today.

5) As Wenamun began and ended his journey within the region of Kharu, an attempt has been made here to define it according to the textual and other evidence. It is clear that travellers entered the lands of Kharu as soon as they left Egypt. Hence the great ym of Kharu may well have been the large expanse of water which lay between Egypt and Lake Timsah, Wenamun's final destination.

6) These proposals with regard to the geographical background of Wenamun's journey appear to be particular ly valid for two reasons: firstly, they lead him to a destination which is still today recognized as El Gibali, consistent with kbn/kpny, if this is indeed derived from gbl. Secondly, and above all, they fit exactly the final detail of this story which tells us that his vessel is blown by the wind off-course to the coast of Irs/Irasa (probably the Alashiya discussed by many scholars until now). We can show that the course we suggest here that Wenamun followed would lead to his being swept upon the shore of Lake Timsah at a place which is still called Arasa/Arashiya today.

Wenamun Reconsidered
Footnotes

1. V. Golenischeff, Receuil de Travaux 21 (1899), 74-102;
A.H. Gardiner, LEM, 61-76. For a list of the translations to
date, see Lichtheim II, 224 and add H. Goedicke,
The Report of Wenamun (1975).

2. Many text-books contain the unfounded assertion that
boats in ancient Egypt were made of cedar. The boat of
Cheops, which is a deep reddish brown in colour, has so far
not been proved to have been made of cedar by analysis of
the boat timbers. It is merely said to be so though the
timber could well be juniper. See AESEN 18f.

3. AESEN Chapter 1.

4. ibid. 5ff. See also Nibbi, Ancient Byblos Reconsidered
(1985).

5. ibid. 2ff.

6. Like Dor, Tyre is thought to be a port along Wenamun's
route simply because it is assumed that he sailed along this
coast. See Golenischeff, cit. 75f.

7. Golenischeff, cit. 77.

8. "The Chief Obstacle to Understanding the Wars of Ramesses
III", GM 59 (1982), 51-60.

9.   This is not discussed in M.L. Bierbrier,
The Late New Kingdom In Egypt (1975) and in K.A. Kitchen,
The Third Intermediate Period (1973) because no-one has ever
suggested that there were any independent city states in
Egypt itself yet it is not beyond the realms of possibility
that this may sometimes have been the case in Egypt.

10. "A note on the Lexikon Entry: Meer", GM 58 (1982), 53-
58; also "A Scientific Challenge to K.A.Kitchen", GM 64
(1983), 7. See also J. Černý in Mélanges Mariette ed. J.
Sainte Fare Garnot (1961), 57-62.

11. No replies have been received with regard to this
challenge except a suggestion that an example might have
existed in the Satrap Stela, a late document of the
ptolemaic period. To this I have now published a reply in GM
69 (1983), 69-80.

12. It is surprising to find Goedicke accepting without
question all the early geographical assumptions with regard
to this story, though he discusses in some detail other
aspects of its content.

13. This is a surprising fact which we may put down to the enthusiasm of the early scholars in attempting to understand the texts.

14. A. Erman, "Eine Reise nach Phönizien im 11. Jahrhundert v. Chr.", ZÄS 38 (1900), 1-18; K. Sethe, "Zur ältesten Geschichte des ägyptischen Seeverkehrs mit Byblos und dem Libanongebiet", ZÄS 45 (1908), 7-35. However, see Nibbi, Ancient Byblos Reconsidered (1985), passim.

15. cit. It must be recalled here that the Hibeh papyri found by Grenfell and Hunt in 1902 of ptolemaic date (third century B.C.) were all from mummy cartonnage, except one: The Hibeh Papyri (1906), introduction to vol. 1. They were not found as a library.

16. Goedicke, cit. 22

17. A.H. Gardiner, Late Egyptian Stories (1932) 76 and 76a. Also Goedicke, cit. 8f.

18. Hieratische Lesestücke II, 29, no. 2

19. See our note 1 above.

20. The full translations available are listed by Lichtheim II, 224 and subsequently also by H. Goedicke in 1975.

21. See Nibbi, "Some Remarks on the god Amun", GM 63 (1983), 53-64. On the cult of Amun, J. Assmann, Re und Amun (1983), Zweiter Teil.

22. This place-name is usually understood to mean Tanis, see AEO II, 172ff

23. This place-name has usually been equated with Dor. However, we must now find an alternative suggestion for it on the inland water route.

24. Goedicke in his commentary p. 28, note m rightly questions the strange form of this name and wonders whether the name of B3djr, usually given as Beder, might not include the name of the town, the first syllable being some kind of title. With regard to the word b3 itself, it is discussed as the name of a Pharaoh of the Third Dynasty in Nabil Swelim's doctorial thesis on this period (University of Budapest, 1981). This term could well be studied further in depth.

25. Lakes, and even ponds, can become very rough in a severe wind. This factor has not been considered with regard to Wenamun's journey or the Story of the Shipwrecked Sailor, yet we have many documents from the early travellers describing the dangers of travelling on the Nile in bad weather, some of which I quote in section viii of this chapter.

26. I believe we have here the Semitic noun rab/rabi, see B. Meissner and W. Von Soden, Akkadisches Handwörterbuch Band II (1972), 933. See Nibbi, Discussions in Egyptology 3 (1985).

27. It is quite clear that Wenamun's credentials are not in order and that he was hoping to be able to act independently for his own temple without political complications. But this foreign ruler was bound to insist upon this formality.

28. The vessel carrying seven logs seems to have been a standard one in the Near East because, besides this reference in the story of Wenamun, it is seen in the reliefs of Khorsabad. There vessels are shown carrying four logs trussed over the heads of the rowers, while three remained floating on the water. See Pritchard ANEP, fig. 107, page 32. The pull of these logs in windtossed waters would be a great hazard to the boat. It is impossible for such vessels to have sailed on the sea.

29. Timber is usually cut in the winter when the tree is dormant and not full of sap as in the growing season. Once a tree is cut and no more water enters its wood from the roots, much of the moisture in the log evaporates and consequently the wood becomes lighter. It also shrinks, mainly around its circumference. Thus a great advantage would lie in carrying logs which had lain on the ground for some time, thus having had time to dry out to some extent. Goedicke does not agree that this happened in the events concerning Wenamun (cit. 141, note 143).

30. Although it was the beginning of the bad season, there would still have been enough water in the Nile channels to get Wenamun and his timber home at the end of the summer. If he felt nervous about the journey at this time and yielded to the temptation of postponing it, there would be no certainty of a Nile high enough the following year to enable him to get home. We must recall here the legend on the map of Lake Timsah in the Description de l'Egypte (Plate 31) which says that in the early years of the nineteenth century, at any rate, Lake Timsah filled with Nile water only in years of high flood. It is conceivable that the envoys of Khaemwese were delayed by a series of low Niles which lasted seventeen years. It may be that the ruler wanted to take no risks with Wenamun's departure. A recent study of historical Nile floods by Fekri A. Hassan may be found in Science Vol. 212, 1142-1145.

31. One might ask whether we do not have here overtones suggesting not only that Wenamun had priestly status, but also perhaps that he was not subject to the Pharaoh in the same way as ordinary citizens.

32. Wenamun's arrival in Alashiya is amazingly sudden and dramatic. He simply tells us that the people immediately came towards him wanting to kill him without giving us any reason for this. We therefore assume it has to do with the hostility he has already engendered along that coastline. It is clear that there is close communication between the princess, the ruler and the people of this area because the dialogue between them is not of a formal nature. If Alashiya was Cyprus, as most scholars suggest, it is unlikely that no reference at all would be made in the text about the journey and its dangers, arrival upon its shore, and an explanation by Wenamun of the events leading to his arrival there. On the other hand, if Alashiya was a stopping place along that same water, it would justify the almost domestic nature of the dialogue recorded for us.

33. Voyage en Egypte 1598 ed. C. and A. Brejnik (1972), folio 39.

34. Voyages en Egypte 1606-10 ed. O. Volkoff (1973), folio 101.

35. Voyage en Egypte 1631 ed. B. Van De Walle (1975), folio 413

36. Voyages en Egypte 1585-1596 ed. O. Volkoff (1976), folios 156-8.

37. Jewish Travellers ed. E.N. Adler (1930),

38. Voyages en Egypte 1589-1591, ed. C. Burri and S. Sauneron (1971), folio 53.

39. Voyage en Egypte 1581 ed. S. Sauneron (1971), folios 45-6, 217.

40. Lettres sur l'Egypte 1785, Vol. I, 71f. See also 274f.

41. Voyage en Egypte 1483 ed. J. Masson (1975), fol. 178b.

42. One Thousand Miles up the Nile (1877), 113f

43. see note 33 above, folio 41.

44. ZÄS 106 (1979), 116-120

45. AESEN Chapter I.

46. ibid. 1ff

47. AEO I, pp 134 and 180.

48. Murray's Classical Atlas ed. G.B. Grundy (1917), Plate I.

114

49. W.G. Waddell, Manetho (1940), pp. 89, 133, 137.

50. See note 41, cit., folio 18 b (p. 42).

51. Voyage en Egypte 1665-6 (ed. C. Libois, IFAO, 1977), fol. 43, p. 95.

52. A Description of the East and Some Other Countries Vol. II, Part I 88f.

53. See GM 58 (1982), 53-58; ibid. 59 (1982), 51-60.

54. AE 148-156.

55. Goedicke, cit. passim.

56. See indexes Vol. II. We have also the excellently reasoned discussion of most of these terms in C. Vandersleyen's Les guerres d'Amosis (1972), but unfortunately he too begins by accepting the traditionally suggested meanings for these terms in examining the evidence.

57. cit.

58. Papyrus Anastasi III, i, lines 9-10. Text in Gardiner, Late Egyptian Miscellanies (1937), hereafter LEM. See also AEO I, p. 181 for Gardiner's discussion on this.

59. See Wreszinski, Atlas II, Plate 39. More recent photographs of these scenes may be found in Karnak 2 vols. by de Miré, Schwaller de Lubicz and Lamy (1982), Plates 32 and 33. Text in KRI I, 6ff. See PM II, 53ff. See also R. Giveon, Les Bédouins-Shosu des documents égyptiens (1971), 56f. While Giveon refers several times to Canaan as a result of the texts, he makes no attempt to define the use of this word or suggest a particular territory for it. We shall limit our comments here by saying that a full discussion and bibliography for this topic, as it may be related to Egypt, is contained in a forthcoming study.

60. On the Sethos I reliefs from Karnak, see A.H. Gardiner, "The Ancient Military Road between Egypt and Palestine", JEA 6 (1920), 99-116, particularly p. 104; also Gardiner AEO II, 202f.

61. Die Ostgrenze Ägyptens (1911), 38ff; AEO II, 202.

62. Egypt in the Classical Geographers (1942), 142, 150, 162.

63. JEA X (1924), 6ff.

64. cit. 104f, following Brugsch.

65. This unique set of reliefs tells us of a campaign in a most concise way, showing the wells at intervals along the base of the relief. These have now crumbled away.

66. A list of the early publications of these scenes may be found in PM II, 53-59.

67. Gardiner, JEA 6 (1920), 104, followed by H. Gauthier, Dictionnaire Géographique D, 95f. We owe this idea to Heinrich Brugsch who, in his Dictionnaire Géographique, 591, 644 and 949-950 based his belief on the assumption that the delta was in ancient times firmly under the control of Pharaoh. The evidence is now increasing to show that this was not so. See also Montet, Géographie de l'Egypte Ancienne II, 200f.

68. H. Halm, Ägypten nach den mamlukischen Lehensregistern, Vol. II (1982), pp. 647 and 693; maps no. 28 and 29 for Tarūt; for Šilla see p.576 and map no. 28.

69. M. Bietak, "Avaris and Piramesse", Proceedings of the British Academy, London, Vol. LXV (1979).

70. AE 137, 148, 240.

71. AEO I, 180ff.

72. AESEN, 102-110.

73. AE, 149-151.

74. Ann. Serv. 42 (1943), 21f.

75. Edel in his masterly analysis of this document in ZDPV 69 (1953), 97-176 with Nachträge in ZDPV 70 (1954), 87. Janssen's article in JEOL 17 (1963), 142f discusses the numbers of these prisoners, and agrees that they are very high.

76. Papyrus Anastasi IV, 17:5. Gardiner, LEM, 54; see also R. Caminos, Late Egyptian Miscellanies (1954), hereafter LEM, 201f.

77. Tuthmosis III, Urk. IV, 670, 694, 707; LD II, 200d; Gardiner, LEM, 62: Urk. II 96:3.

78. AEO I, 180ff.

79. I. Roll and E. Ayalon in PEQ (1981), 111-125.

80. LD III, 126a and b; AEO I, 183; Giveon, cit. 47.

81. Urk.IV, .665: 16.

82. Urk.IV, 712:2.

83. AESEN, 21f.

84. AEO I, p. 183. Also Vandersleyen, cit. 148 f and passim.

85. A.M. Badawy in Ann. Ser. 42 (1943), 1-23.

86. E. Edel commented on the Mitrahina text and compared and collated it with the duplicate from Karnak in ZDPV 69 (1953), 97-176 with Nachträge in ibid. 70 (1954), 87.

87. KRI II, 205-9; PM VII, 102, 39-40.

88. A.H. Gardiner, "Four papyri of the Eighteenth Dynasty from Kahun", ZAS 43 (1906), pp. 31 and 35.

89. Urk.IV, 671. See also W. Helck, Materialien zur Wirtschafts-Geschichte (1961-70), Holz in Index, pp. 1180ff.

90. AESEN, 32-150. In these pages we begin with a discussion of t3 nṯr, the land of god, within which region the land of Punt was situated. An analysis of all the problems concerning a location for Punt follows, and the only answer possible to accept is one which allows for all the evidence to fit together. I believe that my answer is the only one that does this.

91. AESEN 158 and 163.

92. See campaigns nos. 2 and 9 of Tuthmosis III where incense is said to come from Retenu and also from Djahy (campaign 13).

93. Gardiner LEM, 116, Caminos LEM, 431.

94. A. Nibbi, "The Ass and Horse in Ancient Egypt and the Absence of the Mule", ZAS 106 (1979), 148-168.

95. Gardiner, LEM, 84; Caminos LEM, 318.

96. Gardiner, LEM 8; Caminos LEM, 24.

97. Gardiner, LEM, 5; Caminos LEM, 16.

98. Gardiner, LEM 38; Caminos LEM, 138.

99. Gardiner, LEM, 125; Caminos, LEM, 467.

100. AEO I, 185f.

101. Les Nouvelles Fouilles d'Abydos (1896-7), 10-13.

102. Grundriss der akkadischen Grammatik (1952), par. 25, 7
and 8; also Ergänzungsheft zur Grundriss der akkadischen
Grammatik (1969), par. 25d and par. 28a; further discussion
by Von Soden in JNES 27 (1968), 217f and in
Archiv für Orientforschung 19 (1959-60), 149. See also W.
Weidmüller, "Der Buchstabe "K", Entstehung, Entwicklung und
Verbreitung. Mélanges de l'Université de Saint-Joseph 45
(Fasc.16) (1969), 275-293.

103. AESEN 100f, 105f, 121, 122f; GM 69 (1983), 69-80.

104. The Sea Peoples: A Re-Examination of the Egyptian Sources
(1972).

105. GM 69 (1983), 69-80.

106. Many Egyptologists have even now refused to consider
the possibility that the concept of Great Green as Sea is
totally wrong and an unfounded assumption, upon which many
further erroneous ideas are supported. This results in a
very false picture of ancient Egyptian relations with her
neighbours, among other problems.

107. SPE, Chapters 1 and 2.

108. In spite of my longstanding assertion that these were
local rebellions by settled groups along Egypt's borders,
which I first presented in 1972 (see note 104 above), and
also in my The Sea Peoples and Egypt (1975).

109. It is naive to quote the story of Wenamun as evidence
that the ancient Egyptians went to sea, because, if no
example can be found where Great Green or ym indisputably
means sea without the necessity for interpretation, then
they cannot mean sea and Wenamun's journey must be re-
directed inland.

110. AESEN, chapter 1; PEQ 1981, 92.

111. SPE, chapters 2 and 3. See also Nibbi,
Ancient Byblos Reconsidered (1985), passim.

112. ZAS 106 (1979), 116-120.

113. JNES 4 (1945), 45.

114. Lines 2:65-66.

115. Lines 2: 16-19.

116. Voyage en Egypte pendant les années 1587-88 ed. S.
Sauneron. IFAO (1972), page 45.

117. Nibbi in GM 16 (1975), 27-31.

118. Voyage en Egypte 1631 ed. B. van der Walle, IFAO (1975), folio 411.

119. In the early sections of Ancient Byblos Reconsidered (1985) I attempted a definition of the term Djahy, as a compound noun describing the watery nature of the delta region.

120. ibid. contrary to the acceptance by Gardiner, AEO I, 145f, Helck, Beziehungen, 21ff, 267f, 272f, 374ff and Vandersleyen, Guerres, 90-102, 119f, 125f, 200f.

121. AEO I, pp. 132, 134, 148f, 185.

122. H. Gauthier and H. Sottas, Un decret trilingue en l'honneur de Ptolomée IV (1925), 77f where this text is compared to those of Canopus and Rosetta.

123. ibid. 25f.

124. ibid. 25, where Gauthier and Sottas accept Syria for ꜣšr, with which Gardiner seemed to agree. But there is no evidence for this.

125. Urk.II, 131, line 9.

126. Urk.IV, 649.

127. We should examine the literal meaning of these place-names in order to see whether they fit the geographical feature they define before assuming that they must be connected with a remote locality.

128. AEO I, page 134.

129. ibid.

130. AE, 242.

131. GM 16 (1975), 33-38; also Nibbi in JARCE, 13 (1976), 91-95.

132. Urk.IV, 649

133. C. Kuentz, La Bataille de Qadech MIFAO 55 (1928); KRI II, 1-2; A.H.Gardiner, The Kadesh Inscriptions of Ramesses II (1960). See also J. Assman, "Krieg und Frieden im Alten Ägypten: Ramses II. in die Schlacht bei Kadesch", Mannheimer Forum (1983-4); G. Fecht, "Rameses II. und die Schlacht bei Qadesch (Qidsa)", GM 80 (1984), 23-53.

134. <u>GM</u> 59 (1982), 55f; ibid. 64 (1983), 7.

135. See my discussion of the Lebanon (sic) in my <u>Ancient Byblos Reconsidered</u> (1985).

136. <u>AEO</u> I, p. 180f.

137. cit. <u>GM</u> 59, 55f.

138. For the most part, my <u>AESEN</u> was a study of the nḥsj.w as foreigners in ancient Egypt from the Old Kingdom, but <u>not</u> as <u>negroes</u>, for which there is no evidence. See also "The nḥsj.w of the Dahshur Decree of Pepi I", <u>GM</u> 53 (1981).

139. For example, I. Hofmann in <u>GM</u> 46 (1981), 9f.

140. For a summary of our present understanding of <u>w3w3t</u> see Karola Zibelius, <u>Afrikanische Orts- und Völkernamen</u> (1972).

141. <u>Géographie de l'Egypte Ancienne</u> I, 65.

142. listed by Zibelius, cit., note 140.

143. see note 136 above.

144. A reference may be found in G. Vantini, <u>Oriental Sources Concerning Nubia</u> (Heidelberg and Warsaw, 1975), 242; translation from Idrisi in G. Wiet, "Un resumé d'Idrisi", <u>Bulletin de la Societe Royale de Géographie</u>, Vol. XX (1939-1942), 184, with preceding Arabic text. Idrisi tells us that in his day there were extensive ancient ruins at Kūs.

145. See note 137 above. We must not lose sight of the fact that k3š is one of the nḥsj regions which are attested from the Old Kingdom though the name of k3š itself appears only from the Middle Kingdom onwards.

146. British School of Archaeology in Jerusalem, Bulletin no. 4 (1942), 35-45; also ibid. no. 6 (1924), 65ff and ibid. no. 7 (1925), 80ff.

PART II

IRS/ALASA/ALASHIYA

A great deal had been written about this country in the last ninety years, mainly in an unresolved debate assessing the probability of its being either the whole of the island of Cyprus or a part of it, or else a region on the Near Eastern mainland. All this discussion will be considered below and it is listed in a special chronological bibliography at the end of this chapter. It is interesting to note at the outset that we owe the earliest substantial discussion of this topic to several Egyptologists.

i)   Purpose of this discussion

Let me say at once that my own identification set out here revolves around the indisputable fact that there is a place bearing this name today which has until now been ignored. It is marked on our sketch maps figs. 2-5. The geographical facts are such that they indicate a quite extensive region in the past. Any immediate negative reaction to this identification will be due only to the assumptions and preconceived geographical relationships which have been accepted over the last century, without any support from scientific evidence. It will take time to adjust to this physically indisputable reality.

As is often the case, I first found this name on a map while I was looking for something else. I was then as amazed as all scholars will be to find a place of this name situated so closely to Egypt. Yet I was compelled to

122

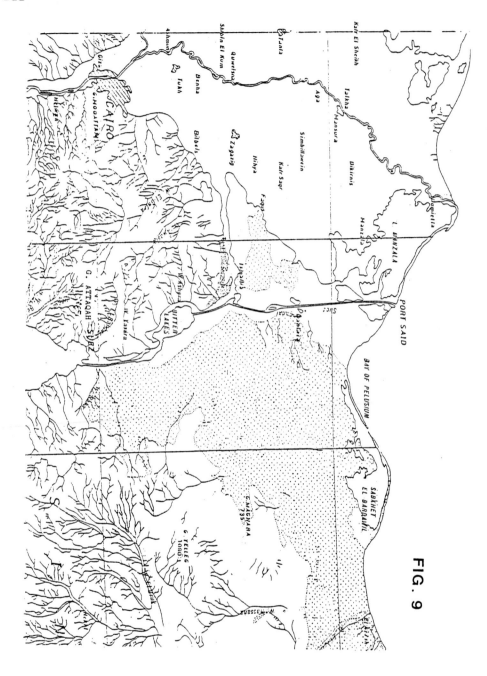

FIG. 9

This sketch shows the drainage system of Gebel Attaqah and
its neighbouring regions. It is drawn from the drainage map
of Egypt based on landsat satellite imagery interpretations
and field investigations, prepared by E. M. El Shazly, M. A.
Abd El Hady and others and published in 1980 by the Academy
of Scientific Research and Technology, Cairo and the
Oklahoma State University, U.S.A.

associate this name with the ancient land of the texts, and the more I thought about it the more it began to make sense. This name was further engraved in my mind when one day, at the market of Ismailia, where the local buses have their terminus, I was looking for a bus to take me to Suez and a bus driver answered me in a loud voice: "Arasha!", meaning that it was a town bus only.

We have already seen how very logically this geographical region fits in with the end of the journey of Wenamun, along inland waters.

A new picture of Irasa/Alashiya will be set out in some detail below, after we have reviewed the existing discussion on this topic so far. Although my main concern here will be to discuss the problem from the point of view of the Egyptian records, over which I have some critical control, I shall attempt also to see whether this locality can answer the needs of the evidence in the literature of the other ancient civilizations of that time, though I am unable to answer for the translation and the interpretation of those texts.

ii) The Name Itself

The Egyptian name in the hieroglyphs is written as in fig. 10 as Irs and may be vocalized Irasa, Arasa or Alasa[1]. As we all know, the l and r are interchangeable in ancient Egyptian and we find that the Egyptian i̧ and present-day European a seem to co-incide, in sound.

a    Tuthmosis III, Urk. IV, 790, no. 213

b    ibid.   791, no. 236   ^cAras ?

c 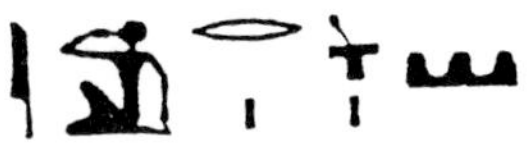   Sethos I, LD III, 131 a

d    Daressy, Rec. Trav. XXXII, 69, no. 23
Ramesses II

e    Ramesses II, Max Mül[l]
Egyptological Resear[c]
II, 91.

f    End of reign of Ram
Papyrus Harris I, [7]

g    Late New Kingdom, Papyrus Anastasi [I]
Plates 15 and 17.

h    Twentieth Dy[nasty]
Wenamun, Rec
Trav. XXI, 98

FIG. 10

The name of Alasiia or Alashiya is vocalized from the Amarna Letters[2] written in cuneiform Akkadian and in other non-Egyptian texts and it is accepted by scholars to be referring to the same place. The reason for this is scientifically acceptable. Amarna Letter 39 bears in the cuneiform text the address of A-la-si-ia as the place of origin and this same letter is endorsed in Egyptian hieratic: "Letter of the Great One of Irs".[3]

It has been suggested that the suffix -iyya often found in Arab names was introduced in our own era[4]. However it appears also in names of other origins in the Near East[5]. Its early appearance in the name of Alasi-ia will eventually oblige scholars to look at it again in an earlier context.

No-one has yet looked carefully enough at the root of this name to see whether anything can be learnt from it. It is important to emphasize that among the many old Egyptian roots[6] which may still be found in modern Berber, we find ers, irsu meaning to descend or put down; irsa (Wargla), a pitch for tents (ers, to pitch). Thus we have the name of Irasa in modern Berber meaning a camping-place or tenting-place. According to the information imparted from our biblical texts, a place chosen to set up camp would imply the availability of fresh water, the existence of natural defences and enough space to pitch the tents in a circle for greater security.

If we look at our map fig. 5. showing the great

length of the Wadi el Arish and the flat nature of the land
along the northern coastline, including the area north of
Lake Timsah, after the very rugged and mountainous regions
to the south, we see what an accurate description of this
area it is to call it Irasa, a place into which people
descended and set up a camp.

It is not impossible that the permanent dwellers in
this area living in tents or huts may have acquired the name
of the area which they have kept to this very day. Karl
Baedeker's guide to Egypt (1929, lxi) says: "There are three
important Beduin tribes in the peninsula of Mount Sinai, the
Terabiyin and the Tiyala who occupy the heart of the
peninsula between Suez and Aqaba, and the Sawarga or
El ^CArayish, to the north of the latter (see fig. 5).

iii) Proof that Isj/Asj/Asjja was not Equivalent to Irs/
     Alasa/Alashiya

Before we review the discussion so far on this topic,
we should eliminate the recurring suggestion that these two
names referred to the same place. We owe this original
suggestion to Wolfgang Max Müller in 1895[7], but, though his
work is still valuable to us, in this he was wrong.

There are at least two topographical lists which
retain still intact the names of both Asija and Irasa, thus
obliging us to accept them as different places. One of these
lists is from the time of Sethos I[8] and other is from the
time of Ramesses II.[9] There are other lists which seem to

have contained both names, but they are damaged[10]. However, it is not only this fact, already emphasized by George Hill and Hector Catling, which suggests that they were different places.

This has also emerged clearly from the discussion by scholars who have listed and compared the products of these two countries[11]. Above all, Asija is said to have produced lapis lazuli and this is never stated to be a product of Irasa/Alashiya, either in the Egyptian texts or in others. We know this to be a rare product so that this should help us to identify Asija. We shall return to this point towards the end of this chapter, after presenting our own case.

W. Von Bissing in 1897[12] could not accept Max Müller's suggestion that both Asija and Irasa referred to Cyprus. If Irasa meant Cyprus, then Asija was more likely to indicate a stretch of the mainland, though he accepted that the exotic products of Asija could be the result of trade.

In 1913, H. R. Hall rightly commented[13] that Asija would never have been identified with Cyprus at all had it not been that in one of the ptolemaic texts, one of the names looks as if it could have been a corrupt form of Asija. Hall believed we could not accept any ptolemaic clues in this respect because, he said rather scornfully, those were the texts which equated Keftiu with Phoenicia!

In a letter to R. S. Merrillees[14], R. O. Faulkner

also stated his belief in 1962 that these texts are speaking of two distinctly different places.

A considerable part of the study of G. A. Wainwright[15] was devoted to a discussion of this problem, though his main interest was archaeological. From this point of view, he could find no objection to treating the two places as one, even though lapis lazuli was said to come from Asija and not from Irasa. He also discusses the fact that lead is also a prominent export from Asija in the texts[16], and concludes on the basis of all the evidence that it cannot represent Cyprus.

A further study on this question by Lynn Holmes appeared in 1982[17]. After examining all the evidence, though unfortunately accepting all the place-names as proved and finally valid, Holmes concluded that there was no real evidence to equate these two places.

The most recent study of Asija was published in 1983 by Wolfgang Helck[18]. As an Egyptologist, he could have re-examined the assumptions underlying the identifications of the names associated with Asija and Alasa, thus giving us a fresh study of the material. However, it was disappointing to find that we have here only a fresh discussion of the old assumptions.

It is abundantly clear from the basic evidence that we cannot equate Asija with Irasa/Alashiya. We shall therefore not be discussing this aspect of the question in our review below. However, we shall be returning to the problems of lapis lazuli and lead, as well as copper, towards the end of this study, after we have outlined what we believe must be accepted as the general territory of Irasa/Alashiya.

iv)   A Chronological Review of the Discussion on Irasa/
      Alashiya

It was Gaston Maspéro who in 1888 first equated the Egyptian toponym Irs with Alasa/Alashiya.[19] Chabas had earlier pinpointed this name[20] but it was not until after the first announcement of the discovery of the Amarna tablets and a first analysis of their contents by A. H. Sayce[21] and E. A. Wallis Budge[22], also in 1888, that it was possible to see the wider-ranging importance of this name. It is also from this early date that Egyptologists have experienced some confusion in separating Irs from the name which is identified as Assur.

In his early, pioneering discussion in 1893 of the places which are named in the ancient Egyptian texts, Wolfgang Max Müller referred to Alasia only briefly three times: pp. 261, 292 and 394.[23] In this work he does no more than identify the texts in which this name is found. But it is clear that already at this time, Irasa was linked by him and by the scholars of his day with the Hittites and was therefore immediately assumed to have been situated in the far north near Kadesh on the Orontes (sic).[24]

It was to be associated with the region called Naharin[25] which also, from this very early period in our studies, was assumed to have been situated in the northern Near East. However, Naharin is another name for which no objective study in depth exists. Scholars have kept repeating these early assumptions without feeling the need to re-examine them. To make matters worse, these unjustified acceptances have been used to make deductions about other placenames related to them. Thus a great confusion was created early in our picture of the geography of ancient Egypt and her immediate neighbours.

The early scholars saw at once that the site for Irasa/Alashiya must be connected to a site where copper was produced and Max Müller believed this to be the area of the Near Eastern coastline directly opposite Cyprus[26], in the first instance. Two years later, however, he changed his mind in a special study of Alasia[27] and said it must be Cyprus. In that study, he centred his attention mainly on the Amarna Letters, as we have all done since then. We find in this article most of the arguments which have been drawn from the texts concerning Irasa/Alashiya and repeated ever since in various languages, without much further clarification. He makes the points that the king of Alasia calls the Pharaoh brother with various possible implications; the land of Alasia bordered upon various territories ridden with political strife, including Hittite territory; Alasia was victim to encroachment of the Lukka people into its territories. Max Müller did not agree that Alasia was necessarily to be equated with the Elisha of Genesis 10:4 and Ezechiel 27:7.

The reason why Max Müller and other scholars at that time concluded that Irasa/Alashiya must be Cyprus is because they believed Cyprus to be the only copper-producing country in that general area.[28] We now know this not to be so.[29] In Max Müller's judgement, and in the judgement of other scholars as well, the other products of Irasa/Alashiya mentioned in the texts were less important. If gold and ivory were not primary products of Cyprus, they were explained as re-shipments, along regular trade routes. The two conclusions are not the result of the same logic.

Max Müller did not neglect to underline the important facts revealed in a number of texts that Irasa/Alashiya produced timber, as well as copper, and that it totally lacked silver. All this was consistent with its being Cyprus, he thought.

It was twenty years later when Wainwright published his very substantial study of this problem.[30] He stressed the fact that copper was plentiful in several sites on the mainland and that copper-working did not have to be identified with Cyprus only. He stressed the fact that the ancient Egyptian qualifying adjective for copper was often stt[31] which is usually accepted as meaning Asiatic, that is western Asiatic. However, from its use in the texts I have now suggested that it probably means simply _imported_.[32]

This scholar also suggested that the exporting of ivory tusks from Irasa/Alashiya fitted in with a mainland site. He quoted the elephant hunt at Niy[33] from the Egyptian records as evidence that elephants were thriving on the Euphrates at that time. However, the suggestion that the place called _Niy_ was situated on the Euphrates is another of the many instant assumptions by the early Egyptologists and is not founded on any evidence at all. It should be borne in mind that elephants in fact never disappeared from Egypt and were being exported from Egypt in quite late times.[34] The elephant is one of the signs of the ancient Egyptian hieroglyphic script which consists of common or everyday animals and objects. However, that is not to say that ivory tusks would not have made a welcome gift at all times, as they do in fact today. The question of the quality of the tusk must also have been important and this would have been related to the environmental factors of its provenance.

Wainwright rightly emphasized that the impression we get from the texts that Irasa/Alashiya was a neutral, almost a buffer state between the Hittites and the Pharaoh was more consistent with its being on the mainland rather than on the island of Cyprus. As to the inscription on an Apollo from Cyprus bearing the title _Alasiotas_[35] Wainwright argued that it was probably imported. He emphasized that there were many examples in Cyprus of imported foreign gods, which he listed for us.[36] This inscription in itself does not compel us to equate Irasa/Alashiya with Cyprus.

With regard to the suggestion by scholars that the biblical Elishah of Ezechiel XXVII, 7 and Genesis X, 4-5 might be Irasa/Alashiya, Wainwright admitted[37] only that it was possible. The texts speak of the isles of Elishah which produced blue and purple, namely the valued dye which was laboriously extracted from the murex shellfish. This would require a position by the sea, whether the actual reference meant isles or coastlands[38].

A further argument against equating Irasa/Alashiya with Cyprus, Wainwright wrote, was the fact that until his own times no traces of cuneiform inscriptions had been found on the island, except in a few clearly imported documents.[39] On the other hand, cuneiform was commonly used on documents from the mainland.

After discussing the difficulties of equating Irasa/Alashiya with Cyprus, Wainwright listed[40] what he considered to be the four indisputable facts relating to this site:
- Her position on the sea-coast;
- Her position as given on the monuments, in which can be included the lands with which she is mentioned in Papyrus Anastasi;
- Her intimacy with Hatti and Sangar, as shown in the Tell el Amarna Letters;

- Her copper trade.

Wainwright emphasized above all that this must have been a maritime country because of the textual references associating it with ships. He does not consider the possibility that these might have been associated with an inland water route, which is the way that I have outlined for Wenamun's journey taking him to Irasa. However it is quite possible that the ancient Irasa/Alashiya included ports on the sea as well as along inland waters as is shown on our sketch map fig.5 which will be discussed below.

The geographical picture of Irasa/Alashiya presented to us by Wainwright and by other scholars after him is based on the contents of some Egyptian geographical lists for which only tentative, exploratory explanations exist even today. Unfortunately scholars have accepted as proven what are no more than suggestions by the early Egyptologists to fit a preconceived picture of the geography and history of ancient Egypt. A discussion of the relationship of Irasa/Alashiya to other places named in the Egyptian documents does not help us even today, because all the identifications so far are all based on circular arguments.

It is to Wainwright's credit that he did not shirk from any of the many problems connected with an identification of this site. Not least is the fact that Amarna Letters 35 and 37 contain requests by the ruler of

Irasa/Alashiya to send <u>silver</u>. In order for such a request
to be made, it must have been an accepted fact at that time
that Egypt could provide silver. This fact alone should make
metallurgists think again before saying that there was no
silver in Egypt in any "marketable" quantity in ancient
times. We shall return to this point towards the end of this
chapter.

Most of our information about Irasa/Alashiya comes
from the Amarna Letters and Wainwright carefully listed the
facts they reveal which might help us to understand the
problem.[41] Besides silver, the ruler of Alashiya asks for an
ox, oils, a bed of gilded <u>usu</u>-wood, several pieces of wood,
a gilded chariot with horses, garments, bed furniture and
various implements.[42] Wainwright was surprised at the
request for one ox and put it down to the fashion of
collecting exotic animals and plants as is suggested by the
reliefs of Tuthmosis III at Karnak which we call the
"botanical garden".[43] However, this reference could well be
to a special variety of humped ox which is portrayed for the
first time in Egypt at the beginning of the Eighteenth
Dynasty in the Masara quarries (Tura, near Cairo).[44] Several
of them are shown harnessed together pulling a stone block
on a sledge. They are not often portrayed and they re-appear
during the time of the so-called invasions of the Sea
Peoples,[45] pulling the carts of the foreigners.

Wainwright stressed that the Amarna Letters make it

clear that the Irasa/Alashiya was not merely a city state, but an important region containing several cities. The fact that the Lukki people could take over city after city over the years, as stated in Letter 38, establishes this as a region, without dispute. Clearly it had a hinterland , including a mountain Taqqata, which produced copper which was supplied to the Hittites.[46] I am suggesting here that the name of Taqqata is the same as Attaqah, one of them having been subject to metathesis. It is shown on our sketch map fig. 9, and will be discussed below in a special section.

It is to Wainwright's further credit that he noted several important characteristics of Irasa/Alashiya from the documents that have come down to us so far. There was a great deal of traffic by both messengers and merchants between Egypt and Irasa/Alashiya while the Alashiyan King seems to have possessed a very detailed knowledge of all their activities, as well as of the events at the Egyptian court. Furthermore, Alashiya had to strive at all times to remain neutral between warring states around her, perhaps furthering in this way her legal system. Wainwright believed that when Wenamun told the female ruler of Alashiya whom he met that he had heard of the justice that was practiced in the land, he may not just have been flattering her to protect himself.[47] It may have been literally true that Irasa/Alashiya had an advanced legal system which protected individual people.

Wainwright's study was based on most of the documents which are still our own main source of information today and his analysis of this problem has remained valid for the most part so far. In spite of the many subsequent discussions of this problem, our basic understanding of it has remained the same since that time.

In his discussion of the oldest name for Cyprus (sic), Fritz Schachermeyer in 1921[48] did not introduce any few factors into the discussion. Like other scholars, he accepted and placed considerable importance on the assumed identification of the placenames in the ancient Egyptian texts and built arguments upon this unstable basis.

Henri Gauthier's lists of the geographical names contained in the ancient Egyptian texts published in 1925 includes Irasa/Alashiya,[49] indicating the views of Egyptologists until that date: Max Müller and Smolenski favouring its identification as Cyprus, Hall in 1922 favouring western Cilicia in support of Niebuhr's views in 1894.[50]

It is a great pity that Claude F.A. Schaeffer in 1951 decided to call his Cyprus site Enkomi-Alasia before the general debate on this was resolved on a scientific basis to the permanent satisfaction of all scholars. To make matters worse, his Volume IV is called simply Alasia (Mission Archeologique d'Alasia). This is going to be very awkward for us all if it is proved in time scientifically that _Alasia_ cannot have anything to do with Cyprus on the basis of the evidence available.

Unfortunately, Schaeffer's impetuous example was followed by others and one cannot but regret that much of the energetic analytical work on the ancient history of the Near East has been based on the unproved assumption that Irasa/Alashiya was Cyprus, thus rendering it useless to us.

The Egyptologists Jean Yoyotte[51] (1949), Jean Vercoutter[52] (1956) and Wolfgang Helck[53] (1962) all accepted Irasa/Alashiya as Cyprus, the latter quoting as his grounds the footnote by Yoyotte and the list compiled by Gauthier in 1925. But clearly no solution was possible from a study of the ancient Egyptian texts alone.

When he discussed this problem in 1950, Anton Jirku concluded that an objective study of the material showed that Irs/Alashiya must be located in the north of Syria.[54] He placed considerable weight on the Ugaritic document from Ras Shamra containing the names of families which carried a marginal note "town of Alashiya". He concluded rightly that this must be a neighbouring country and not a remote and comparatively inaccessible island.

In Kadmos I (1962), Gerd Steiner discussed some "new" texts concerning Irasa/Alashiya, namely those which had come to light around that time in archives from Hittite sources and also from Ugarit, Mari and Alalakh.[55] This scholar

underlines a new fact. Among the products of Alashiya,
copper is named only second to gold in one Hittite document
from Boğazköy, demanding tribute from this land. Thus gold
must have been considered as a product of Irasa/Alashiya at
that time.

The other point emphasized by Steiner at this stage
of the discussion is the report of a battle between the
Hittites and Alashiya in the middle of a water which is
interpreted by him as sea. The word accepted here as sea is,
I am told, by no means proved beyond doubt. The general
literary context gives no indisputable example of this. It
would be helpful to know how the Hittites referred to their
lakes and inland waters, before we accept that their battle
took place on the sea. However, it will not upset the case
we shall present below if this word is eventually proved
to mean sea in the course of time. What is most upset by the
interpretation of this word as sea, and the event as a Sea
Battle, is the logic of the whole history of the Hittites
who are not easily to be associated with the sea. However,
we must bear in mind my earlier remarks with regard to
Wenamun, whose story certainly can be explained very
satisfactorily by having him sail on an inland water.

Some of the "new" broken texts quoted by Steiner read
very much like the so-called Treaty between Egypt and the
Hittite countries during the reign of Ramesses II.[56]

Steiner indicated from these texts that

Irasa/Alashiya was probably an island[57], a point taken up later with fresh evidence and greater conviction by Olivier Masson[58]. This is acceptable in our view, though only if we bear in mind the fact that islands occur on lakes and inland waters, as well as in the sea.

In 1967, Hans Güterbock[59] carefully considered Gerd Steiner's analysis of the "new" documents and he found himself in disagreement with some of those views. He concluded that it was not yet clear how the sea victory (sic) of Suppiluliumas II would fit into the history of his time and it was better to wait until the Ras Shamra documents were published in full.

Güterbock remarked that the publication of some of these texts do not make it clear how the various warring sides are made up.[60] He emphasized that whereas the texts from Ras Shamra depict Alashiya as an ally of Ugarit, and by implication, of the Hittites, Suppiluliumas is said to be fighting "the enemies from Alashiya". It is not clear whether this means that the whole country had joined these enemies, or whether it was only partly occupied by an enemy. Nor is it clear whether this enemy had anything to do with the enemy to whom the sailors of Ugarit are said to have handed their vessels.[61]

Very important in this discussion has been the study of Cyprus by Hector Catling for the Cambridge Ancient History,[62] in which he includes a brief section on Irasa/Alashiya, as far as the evidence can take him. Speaking as an expert on Cyprus, which no-one will dispute, he concisely lists for us the reasons why it is unlikely that Irasa/Alashiya was Cyprus or a part of it. Although there are some grounds for supporting that identification, there is no certainty about it. Catling points out that Cypriot objects are extremely rare in Hittite lands[63]. Moreover, though Cyprus was literate in the Late Bronze Age, no traces of the use of cuneiform can be found. Yet the Alashiya chancellery was fluent in Akkadian and was able to use cuneiform.[64] Catling rightly emphasized that the copper that was demanded as tribute from Alashiya has been given undue prominence, because there were other sources of copper besides Cyprus. He also pointed out that the items of tribute may not necessarily have originated in that country. On this I tend to disagree, because it does not make a great deal of sense to make demands of regular tribute of a particular product from a country when that product has to come from somewhere else. I believe it is most rational to accept that when a demand was made from a country, the ruler making that demand must have believed it to be possible.

For this reason the demand for elephant tusks makes it unlikely that Irasa/Alashiya could have been Cyprus, though it is conceivable that there may have been an international trade in these.

There are also those scholars who believe that Cyprus
must have been named in the ancient documents and that
therefore Irasa/Alashiya is the most likely ancient name for
it. It is Catling's belief that it is doubtful whether
Cyprus had achieved an appropriate degree of importance by
the time the Amarna Letters were written. He concludes very
reasonably that this identification should be regarded as
unproven until fresh evidence is available.

Quite remarkably, Catling's rational and properly
cautious view did not appeal to many scholars, who produced
a variety of totally irrational views and counter-arguments.
One of these was M. J. Mellink[65] whose review in 1968 of
Catling's remarks on Alashiya is based on pure phantasy and
has no relationship at all to scientific fact. This includes
his statement that "the map of the eastern Mediterranean
coast and of Syria is beginning to become fairly well-known,
at least in a relative topographical sense and nothing
points to Alashiya's being a Cilician or Syrian site".
Catling had not suggested either of these things. Moreover,
the sad fact is that we shall never have a full picture of
this area because many of the ancient city-states on their
mounds have now been either bull-dozed or blasted away,
leaving no trace.

It was extremely disappointing to find H. Otten[66]
expressing his belief in the equation of Alashiya/Cyprus, or
a part of Cyprus, on the grounds, as he stated, that it was

no longer disputable (sic) in spite of the careful analysis of this problem by Hector Catling.

In 1971, Y. Lynn Holmes[67] made some further comments on this problem, he too having made a special study of Cyprus. These were centred mainly on the contents of the non-Egyptian texts concerning Alashiya and indicating a possible location for it, which he believed must be Cyprus or some part of it.[68] He emphasizes several points which had not been touched upon before. Firstly, he stressed that two texts referring to Alashiya indicate that it was a place of exile. This leads him to believe that Cyprus would best satisfy this requirement. Furthermore two letters from Ugarit suggest that Alashiya was situated in a place from which the invaders of Ugarit could be seen before they arrived there. At the same time, they reveal that the Alashiyan king did not have the knowledge of the movement of Ugaritic ships, chariots and troops.[69]

Lynn Holmes comments that if Alashiya had been north of Ugarit, it would have been unlikely that the king of Alashiya would not have known what was happening in that country. However, he suggested, if Alashiya had in fact been Cyprus, this would not have been suprising. But surely this would also have been the case if Alashiya had been situated on the mainland south of Ugarit!

Furthermore, this scholar asks, if Alashiya had been situated in Cilicia or in northern Syria, why should there have been so few references to it in the Hittite texts? If Alashiya were to be equated with Cyprus, this fact was understandable.

Lynn Holmes also refers to the so-called naval battle as a very important clue to this problem.[70] This would certainly be the case if we could be absolutely certain about all the circumstantial facts. But we can not. This scholar himself acknowledges that a sudden naval success on the high seas by a non-maritime people like the Hittites is a very strange report in itself.

This scholar followed up this study with some further comments in 1982,[71] in which he discussed the Egyptological material. Necessarily, this involves a discussion of the place-names with which Irasa/Alashiya is associated. We have already described the circumstances in which these names assumed instant identification very early in our Egyptological studies. Instead of doubting our understanding of the lists and the contexts in which this name is found, Lynn Holmes very unwisely expresses his doubts on the geographical accuracy of the lists and the texts themselves.[72] Like many other scholars in this, as in other problems, no thought was given to the accuracy of the basis upon which the case was to be argued. Such a thought was all the more remote because investigation needed to be carried out in another discipline.

The Proceedings[73] of a colloquium on ancient Cyprus, published in Nicosia in 1972 contains two studies on Alasia, one by R.S. Merrilles and the other by J.D. Muhly.

Merrillees[74] argues against the possibility of Irasa/Alashiya's being Cyprus, or even a part of it. He emphasizes that there is no evidence for any but the most sporadic commercial contacts between Cyprus and her neighbours until the MC III period, when comparatively more substantial exports of pottery to the Levant began to take place. He also emphasizes that the first time this name is mentioned in the Egyptian hieroglyphs is in the Eighteenth Dynasty, even though contacts with Egypt had been in existence for a century beforehand and were soon to enter into a decline. Furthermore, whereas neither Enkomi nor any major Late Cypriote coastal city has until now produced any articles of trade inscribed with the name of Tuthmosis III or any significant deposits of imported Egyptian goods belonging to this period, there is much evidence on the mainland at Ras Shamra and its port for close links with Egypt in the first half of the 15th century B.C., Merrillees noted[75] that not even Ugarit is mentioned in the lists of Tuthmosis III though it is doubtful whether we know the correct name for that city.[76] This scholar also underlined the fact that the Amarna Letters were written in Akkadian on clay tablets in cuneiform script. The site of Alasia should therefore produce some evidence of this writing. Yet Cyprus has produced only four tablets in the Cypro-Minoan script, all from Enkomi, whereas Ras Shamra on the mainland has produced a great quantity of such documents. Though clearly Ras Shamra cannot have been Alasia, the city bearing that name must closely have resembled ancient Ugarit.[77] Merrillees concludes by suggesting that Alasia may have been situated on the Gulf of Iskenderun, on one of its major mounds, because the circumstantial evidence favours this site best.[78]

J.D. Muhly's paper[79] in this Cyprus colloquium came out in favour of identifying Irasa/Alashiya with Cyprus or Enkomi. He followed Schaeffer's impetuous lead in accepting this[80] and said that this identification "has come to be regarded as an established fact", even though the debate is by no means over for lack of conclusive evidence either way.

He goes on to attack Catling[81] for opposing this identification without proposing any alternative location, as if the latter fact invalidated the former. Catling had gone against the current view, he said, and for this reason must be wrong. Mellink is quoted as the explicit upholder of the current belief and Muhly expresses his agreement with him "that there does not seem to be room for a kingdom of Alashiya apart from the island of Cyprus"!

Muhly considered this to be a sound basis for his belief because he goes on to remark: "Attempts to suggest precise locations in Syria, such as Kinet Huyuk, north of Ras Shamra, are obviously based upon pure speculation and are of little value without some sort of confirmation through excavation."[82]

Muhly goes on to dismiss the arguments recognizing Semitic characteristics in the language of the Amarna Letters and the fact that they are written in Akkadian cuneiform. He emphasizes that there is no evidence of the use of cuneiform in Egypt either, apart from the chance finds at Amarna.[83] He says that the isolated dialect elements found in the Amarna Letters are not extensive enough to provide an argument for any location. It would in any case not be suprising, he said,[84] to find Canaanite (sic) influence in Cyprus as well, and one of the more recently published letters from Alashiya seems to betray the influence of Mycenaean Greek.[85]

Muhly insists that the arguments of Catling and others against the identification of Irasa/Alashiya as Cyprus or a part of it suggest that the case for it is not understood. He goes on to discuss what he considers to be the basic points in detail.

Firstly he emphasizes the date of the earliest reference to Irasa/Alashiya which shows close contact with Mari[86]. This means that in the first half of the eighteenth century B.C. the Syrian site of Mari was importing copper from Alashiya, some texts referring to the mountain of Alashiya, which is named Taggata in the Hittite texts.[87] In view of the fact that copper smelting

was known to have occurred in Cyprus at least as early as
the latter part of the third millennium, Muhly believes that
it can be accepted as a working hypothesis that Cypriot
copper was being exported to Mari at that time.[88]

Very unfairly, Muhly accuses Catling of not giving
sufficient attention to the contents of the Ugaritic texts
in his "survey of the Alashiya problem".[89] But Catling's
study was dealing with the archaeology of Cyprus and his
task required him to do no more than to consider the problem
of Irasa/Alashiya within that context alone. This he did
rationally and succinctly, taking account of what little
evidence there was.

Though not himself a linguist specializing in the
Ugaritic texts, Muhly gives us an extensive analysis of
their contents with comparisons between these and those from
Alalakh and the Hittite areas. He shows no hesitation in
accepting the translations of those texts and the
topographical and other names contained in them. He goes so
far as to instruct us that some of those names are "Semitic
and Anatolian",[90] though he may be right in emphasizing that
the inhabitants of Alashiya are listed together with
Hittites and Hurrians in the Ugaritic texts.[91]

The Ugaritic text UT 2008[92] suggests that Baal,
Astarte and Anath are the gods of Irasa/Alashiya, but Muhly
re-interprets this for us enabling him to affirm that the
text says "absolutely nothing regarding any specific deities

worshipped in Alashiya".[93]

Further criticism is levelled at Catling with regard to his reference to Egyptian sources[94]. Here Muhly's understanding of what Catling actually said is wrong and so is his information concerning the Egyptian material. Muhly said that the principal complication in dealing with the Egyptian texts is the existence of two names, Isy and Irs, both of which have been taken as references to Alashiya. However, he failed to understand Catling's point that the two names appeared together on one list,[95] thus compelling us to treat the two as separate entities. In fact, as I have already pointed out [96], there are two such lists extant and others which are damaged, yet suggesting that there were probably other examples as well.

Whenever the texts from the time of Tuthmosis III refer to Isy or Asy or Asija, all vocalizations being possible, they are referring to a land which is certainly not Irs or Irasa/Alashiya. Muhly dismisses Catling's statement of fact by quoting his feelings on the matter: "It is not possible to go into all the arguments here. Suffice it to say it is now felt that both names refer to Alashiya".[97]

When Muhly quotes examples of this name[98] from the Egyptian Papyrus Anastasi IV he, like most scholars, sees these references in a context associated with far-flung foreign parts, such as Babylonia and the Hittite lands. But

we are bound to repeat here yet again that these
identifications are no more than assumptions which have
remained unproved and unquestioned until now. Muhly compares
the description in Papyrus Anastasi IV of children carrying
ingots of metal upon their necks with the tomb paintings
showing ox-hide ingots being brought into Egypt by
foreigners[99] and he comments upon the fact that the name of
Alashiya is never mentioned on those wall-paintings.

It is to be regretted that the interpretation of the
Egyptian historical texts is distorted by the fact that we
do not properly understand the names of places contained in
them. For this reason any analysis of the Alashiya problem
which needs to take these into account is completely useless
to us.[100] Yet it is on this foundation that Muhly
concludes[101] that Alashiya can only be the island of Cyprus.
If our lack of understanding of the Egyptian documents were
matched by a similar uncertainty in the texts from other
sources, then most of the arguments for or against the
equation of Irasa/Alashiya with Cyprus should be set aside.

It was quite astonishing to find Hara Georgiou in
1979[102] beginning her paper by rejecting Catling's
indisputable and factual case and accepting the fanciful
arguments of Mellink and Muhly[103] that Cyprus was Alashiya,
supported by the meek capitulation to this idea by Heinrich
Otten[104]. She begins this paper from this point of view and
indeed at times her use of the term Alashiya for Cyprus

creates some confusion in her discussion. The main thrust of her paper is to show that the Late Bronze Age evidence from Cyprus itself supports its identification with Alashiya.

She emphasizes that one of the earliest literary references to Alashiya is contemporary with the first of the new Middle Cypriot II contacts with the east. Hara Georgiou agreed with Catling that contact between Cyprus and the east increased considerably in MC III and LC I.

We are given a graphic description of the content of the Hittite texts referring to Alashiya[105] though it is acknowledged that the detail of these events is not available to us. Among the facts that seem to be clear from these texts is that Alashiya was used as a place of banishment by the Hittites.[106] Unfortunately, assumptions are made to fill the gaps and to explain the events. There is no explanation as to why this scholar tells us that "Alashiya was politically subordinate in terms of actual power to both Egypt and the Hittites."[107]

The discussion of the Egyptian material by Hara Georgiou falls into the same trap as we have already seen in other cases. She assumes that all the translations and the identifications of places are proved and beyond doubt, whereas they are not. She too, like other scholars, makes much of the story of Wenamun. However, we believe that our own picture of this journey presented here in an earlier chapter must be considered by scholars, because it makes much more sense than the old one, and confirms the comparative intimacy of the ancient world.

In 1979, we saw the appearance of Lennart Hellbing's thesis devoted to the problems concerning Irasa/Alashiya.[108] He presents a methodical and painstaking study of all the aspects of this problem, carefully annotated and indexed. So fairly did he weigh his arguments that in the end he cannot himself take one side or the other. Because it is a summary of all the arguments and all the material upon which the discussion has taken place, it makes an excellent reference book.

Though we must be grateful for his effort, its very impartiality prevents him from bringing any spark of freshness or conviction to it.

It is also unfortunately true that when a scholar attempts to base his work on several disciplines, even with excellent advice available to him, his ideas are bound to be filtered. He is building his structure on insecure foundations, because he is depending on the interpretation by others of the original material. I see this to be particularly true with regard to the Egyptological texts.

I shall be referring to Hellbing's work in detail when I am presenting my own case further on.

In 1980, John Strange went over this ground again with reference to his discussion of Caphthor/Keftiu [109], he too using sources from several disciplines. In summarizing all the arguments for both sides,[110] he takes the position that Alashiya cannot have been the whole island of Cyprus, but that it was more likely to have been a site on the mainland.

At a congress on the history and archaeology of Salamis in Cyprus in 1978[111] we find Jean Leclant not only upholding the view that Irasa/Alashiya was Cyprus, but also that Isy and Irs perhaps were the same. He reads Salamis in a crucial section of the Canopus decree[112] but all this ground is covered in a very short space and rests on what I believe to be many traditional but unproved arguments.

v)   A New Geographical Concept for Irs/Arasa/Alashiya

The area of Ismailia which borders upon the northern shore of Lake Timsah is still today called Arashiya. To the west of it, there is an area still called Arashiya El Qadima (see our fig. 5 here). In addition to this we have other evidence which suggests that this name applied to a fairly extensive region. We have an ancient wadi with its outlet upon the Mediterranean Sea bearing the name of El Arish. This is quite literally Irs/Arasa. Furthermore, west of El Arish, we have a town called El^{C}Aras (see our sketch map fig. 5.) which I believe to be the same name, affected by local variation. We also find a town of this same name west of Bilbeis.[113]

It is not unlikely that the whole region which

154

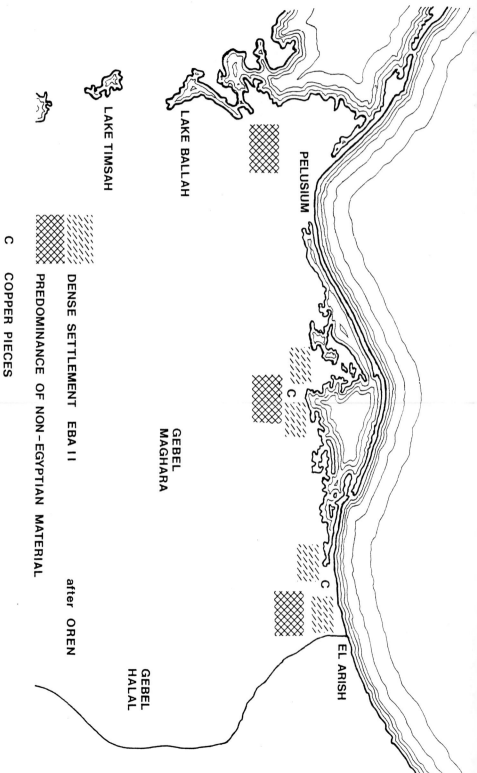

FIG. 11

LAKE TIMSAH

LAKE BALLAH

PELUSIUM

GEBEL
MAGHARA

C

GEBEL
HALAL

EL ARISH

C

C

DENSE SETTLEMENT EBA II

PREDOMINANCE OF NON-EGYPTIAN MATERIAL

C   COPPER PIECES

after OREN

includes this surviving name in various forms constituted the lands of the ancient Irs/Arasa/Alashiya which are referred to in the ancient documents of several northern neighbours of Egypt. The minor variations which we find in the name today suggest that in the course of time, the region became fragmented and the places bearing this name, isolated.

There is a reference in the biblical texts to Alush, the same name, as a camping-place situated in a fertile area of the Sinai, as the people of Israel left Egypt: Numbers 33: 13-14. The geographical site for this place in the vicinity of the Sinai area is confirmed indirectly in Exodus 17:1; 19:2. It is interesting to note that the biblical texts describe it as a camping-place, just as the Berber root for this word suggests. We drew attention to this at the beginning of this chapter.

Finally we must not lose sight of the fact that the Wadi El Arish collected water from a very wide area or basin which covered more than half of the Sinai peninsula (see our sketch map fig. 5).

The absolute proximity of Irs/Arasa/Alashiya to the ancient Egyptian border, so far south, will undoubtedly be very disconcerting for most of us but is a reality that we shall have to accept in time. Today that area is a part of Egypt. This identification will affect two fundamental facts concerning the Near East in ancient times.

FIG. 12 a

FIG. 12 **b**

Firstly, we shall have to accept thè Hittite occupation of territory upon Egypt's very doorstep. No-one so far had thought that their presence had penetrated overland so far south. From the Egyptological point of view, this is a welcome discovery because it makes Egypt's relationship with the Hittites much more cogent and real. It had always worried me that the Hittite Treaty of Ramesses II conveyed the idea that the two countries were adjacent to each other while no real evidence for this could be found. Many Egyptian references to the Kheta suggest that they not only knew the people, but also their lands. Thus the Egyptian texts will now be given fresh meaning and the possibility of more accurate understanding.

The recent finds in Tell ed Daba north by the Hildesheim Pelizaeus Museum team, led by Dr. Pusch, include a shield mould of the shape that we see held by the Kheta warriors on the Egyptian relief. We look forward to the forthcoming publication of their preliminary announcement. We must emphasize here however, that this shape of shield is never seen in the iconography from Hittite lands in Asia Minor (see fig. 12 here). Should we perhaps now begin considering the Kheta evidence quite independently from our acceptance of this name as indicating Hittites?

Secondly, if this identification of

Irs/Alasa/Alashiya is right, it will finally belie the repeated assumption by some scholars that Egypt's ancient Empire reached the Euphrates. There has never been any evidence for saying this and now, the continuing presence of Irs/Alasa/Alashiya on Lake Timsah will be a positive obstacle to such an assertion. We are getting closer to the truth. The fact that the ancient people themselves came to Egypt proves beyond doubt the influence and attraction which the Nile culture held for them and in no way diminishes the power which Egypt exerted during those times.

vi) Our Limited Archaeological Picture for Arashiya

As usual, we find that the archaeological information for these areas is scanty.[114] We are fortunate, however, in having the survey of 1972 by E. D. Oren and others of the area between Pelusium and El Arish. Oren called it "the overland route between Egypt and Canaan". We must emphasize the absence of any scientific definition for the land or the people or the culture of Canaan so that we must for the moment reject the use of this term in that survey for which we are nevertheless very grateful.

Their aim was to record all the ancient sites in this area, to clarify their nature against the background of their geography and to examine the cultural contacts between Egypt and her neighbours in the period prior to the Graeco-Roman. The information we have of these areas is very fragmentary, even now. The team divided the area into sections and recorded over 250 sites ranging from the

Chalcolithic period to the Middle Ages. They found the most intensive periods of occupation to have been the Early Bronze Age I-II, the Late Bronze Age, the Graeco-Roman period and the early Islamic period.[116]

They found the earliest settlement, and also the most densely-populated, to have been an area close to El Arish (see sketch map fig. 11). There some fifty sites were recorded over an area of ten kilometres, at distances of between 50 and 400 metres apart. A similar distribution was noted in areas further west showing a very heavy settlement on the many dunes along the coastline. Evidence of habitation was found on the western and north-western slopes of these dunes and in shallow depressions between dune ridges, for protection against the prevailing winds.

Although no architectural remains were encountered the discovery of stone tools and the remains of cooking installations suggested that they were more than seasonal encampments. Morever, their density reveals that they were not merely temporary stations along an old trade route. Furthermore, Oren found[117] that the size, location and distribution of these early sites very closely resembled those of present-day Beduin settlements. He commented that it was not unlikely that the same way of life has prevailed in this region throughout its history, with both seasonal and permanent encampments side by side with large villages.

Throughout the whole area, the proportion of Egyptian

materials found predominated over the Canaanite (sic) in the ratio of 5:1. However, there were some sites in the areas marked on our sketch map fig. 11 where it was the non-Egyptian material which predominated. In recording the detail of this pottery[118] Oren remarked that the greatest number of Egyptian sherds found were of the First Dynasty while some could be assigned with certainty to the late pre-dynastic. The non-Egyptian material consisted of Chalcolithic and Early Bronze I-II types. This particular mixture of pottery, which seems to be common also in a number of sites of southern Palestine, suggested to Oren that the material culture of the First Dynasty of Northern Sinai and of Southern Palestine should be viewed as one related phenomenon. In these areas there seems to have been a complete absence of Egyptian material of the Second Dynasty and later, to be resumed only around the Sixth Dynasty.[119] We cannot agree with Oren that this means that the communications between Egypt and her neighbours became waterborne during this time. Nor can we agree that his evidence suggests that Egypt used the northern Sinai "as a spring-board forcing her way into Canaan". We hope to show in a forthcoming study that Canaan extended also into the delta of Egypt.

In a survey based on the excavation of four sites in South Sinai[120] Itzhak Beit-Arieh found settlement clusters which could be related only to EB II in the vicinity of copper mines. He found the material culture of this occupation to be non-Egyptian and in fact identical to the EB II culture of Arad. It is interesting that the clay source for the common cooking pots at Arad 1-111 is the granite area of central, south Sinai. There appear to be further strong analogies between these sites in the south Sinai and Arad in the character of the flint tools, the copper axes and square-sectioned copper borers, stone pendants and shell "buttons". There were also architectural features linking the two areas.

There was little evidence of Egyptian activity in these areas, particularly near the copper mines. This confirms what Egyptologists have long accepted that the pursuit of copper in this territory was not an Egyptian activity, though all will accept the strong evidence for their presence in Serabit El Khadim and Maghara along the western Sinai, where turquoise abounded.

A more recent survey by Itzhak Beit-Arieh of Serabit El Khadim has now appeared.[121] This flat-topped mountain rising to a height of approximately 800 metres above sea-level contains many concentrations of turquoise and Beit-Arieh counted more than twenty ancient mines in this area, the earliest dating from the Third Dynasty reign of Sekhemkhet while the last king to have mined turquoise in this area seems to have been Ramesses VI of the Twentieth Dynasty.

The most interesting find in mine L was an intact

metallurgical workshop, which contained 47 stone casting-moulds as well as other equipment. There was evidence that casting activity was carried out on the site, particularly for the tools used in the mining activity itself. Beit-Arieh includes photographs and drawings of the finds which are most important for us all.

What is very clear from all the Sinai reports is that the ancient Egyptians seem never to have been directly concerned with the mining of copper which they appear to have imported from neighbouring territories, including the Eastern Desert, in early times. The evidence suggests that the Eastern Desert was also a foreign country for Egypt during the pharaonic period.

vii)   How this geographical identification of Irs/Arasa/
       Alashiya fits in with the evidence from the Egyptian
       documents.

We shall refer here to the ancient Egyptian documents which mention Irs, excluding the Amarna letters, which will have a special section of their own immediately following this.

A comprehensive list of the ancient Egyptian texts in which this name occurs was drawn up in 1915 by G. A. Wainwright in his fundamental article to which we have already referred several times. In this, he also listed how the name was written in each case.[122] There was a further discussion of these examples in Lynn Holmes's review of the "Isj-Ars" controversy in 1982[123], though his protestation at the writing of this name in the time of Tuthmosis III,[124] thus rendering it doubtful, he believed, cannot be upheld scientifically. Nor can his unquestioning acceptance of the so far unproved identification of the names associated with Irs in the geographical lists, which influence his judgement as to its location. In this Lynn Holmes is not alone. Too much weight has been given by all non-Egyptologists to these assumed identifications, by treating them as though they were proved beyond all doubt, whereas this is far from true.

The earliest example we have identified so far for the name of Irs dates from the time of Tuthmosis III. However, taking into account the dense settlement of this area in the Early Bronze Age and its close proximity to Egypt, it seems impossible that we should have no reference to it in earlier times. It is quite probable that it was referred to by another name before the New Kingdom.[125]

For our own convenience we list here chronologically the passages in which the name of Irs occurs, mindful of the fact that at the beginning of this chapter we set out the reasons why we believe it to be impossible that Isj/Asj should be equated with Irs. Wainwright's list not only included Isj/Asj, but also some damaged examples of Irs. We shall not list the latter here, because they do not affect the argument in any way.

We have the following occurrences of the name Irs in the ancient Egyptian texts:

1. <u>Tuthmosis III</u>. Temple of Amun at Karnak, north-east façade of seventh pylon, list of defeated enemies from the north. <u>PM</u> II, 167f. This list contains two names which may be read as <u>Irs</u>, see <u>Urk.IV</u>, 790, no. 213 and ibid. 791, no. 236, the latter perhaps ^c<u>Aras</u> ? (see our fig. 10 b here). There are some slight variations in the writing of this name.

2. <u>Sethos I</u>. Temple of Sethos I at El Gurna (Thebes), Inscription on sphinx in first pylon, in a geographical list of defeated enemies. <u>LD</u> III, 131a; <u>KRI</u> I, 33 no. 12; <u>PM</u> II, 408.

3. <u>Ramesses II</u>. Stela of Amenhotep, BM 166, referring to a woman from <u>Irs</u>, published by J. Lieblein, <u>Dictionnaire des noms hiéroglyphiques</u>, (1871), no.888.

4. <u>Ramesses II</u>. Stela fragment, no name, at Freiburg in Baden, no. 104, referring to a man from <u>Irs</u>. A. Wiedemann, <u>PSBA</u> XIII (1980), 31f; <u>KRI</u> III, 846.

5. <u>Ramesses II</u>. Reliefs referring to mining activity, in which <u>Isj/Asj</u> and <u>Irs</u> are listed in immediate sequence, first published by W. Max Müller, <u>Egyptological Researches</u> II, 90ff. See also <u>KRI</u> II, 620.

6. <u>Ramesses III</u> Medinet Habu, Mortuary Temple of Ramesses III, Inscription of Year 8 lists <u>Irs</u> among the enemy (so-called Sea Peoples). Oriental Institute, University of Chicago, Plate 46, line 17; also <u>KRI</u> V, 39f.

7. <u>End of reign of Ramesses III</u>. Papyrus Harris, now in British Museum, historical section, Plate 75, line 4 tells us that a man called <u>Irsw</u>, <u>a man from Kharu</u>, arose as chief

among the foreigners in the land of the Black City. S. Birch:

Facsimile of the Egyptian Hieratic Papyrus of the Reign of Ramesses III (1876). Hieroglyphic version by W. Erichsen, Papyrus Harris I (1933); publications listed by D. Jankuhn, Bibliographie der Hieratischen und Hieroglyphischen Papyri (1974), 48f. Translation into English BAR IV, par. 398 in particular. See our fig. 10 f for writing of name of Irsw.

8. Late New Kingdom. Papyrus Anastasi IV, now in the British Museum (BM 10249) contains some non-political references to Irs which are to some extent enlightening. We find them among lists concerning domestic trade:

15:2   ḏft-oil of Irs

15:3   jnb-oil of Irs

17:8   dḥw-metal on the neck of the children of Irs

17:9   cows of Irs

Gardiner LEM 34-56; Caminos LEM 125-221, for translation.

9. Twentieth Dynasty, Papyrus of Wenamun, now in Moscow Museum. At the end of this story, when Wenamun finally leaves kbn/kpnj with his load of timber, he is blown off course by a fierce wind to the shore of Irs. V. Golenischeff, Rec. Trav. XXI (1899), 98. Annotations by Gardiner in his Late Egyptian Stories (1932). See also M. Lichtheim AEL II, 229 and H. Goedicke, The Report of Wenamun (1975), who both accept the traditional geographical picture for this journey. This story tells us a great deal about life and conditions in the areas bordering upon the Nile and

the delta but the basic problem is to identify the route of the journey and the identity of the recurring place-names.

I have attempted to do this in our earlier chapter on Wenamun, including his arrival in Irs by water.

As we have already said, our list does not include the damaged contexts which are listed by Wainwright as his examples 13 and 16, and we omit as doubtful his example 21 from a text from Aniba, LD III, 229c. See also Steindorff, Aniba II, Plate 101 and p. 243 as well as PM VII, 76 for a background of this inscription. It is odd to find that Lynn Holmes adds a man among the determinatives for this example (his note 50, p. 333).

Our list above also includes, under no. 7, an example not listed by others so far, but one which I believe firmly belongs in this list. Remarkably, the man from Irs in this context is described also as being a man from Kharu. This appears to agree with our description of Kharu, as far as the texts would allow us, in our earlier discussion of the story of Wenamun. We suggested there that this name was linked to the waterways flowing eastwards in the eastern delta. Furthermore, we must emphasize that Wenamun's journey to kbn/kpnj, where he obtained his timber, remained within the lands of Kharu, so that when his vessel was blown off-course immediately upon leaving kbn/kpnj, he was still within the area of Kharu when he was blown on to the shore of Irs, present-day Arashiya, as we have already proposed.

Thus the man from Irs called Irsw in the Papyrus Harris, was
also a man from Kharu, who seems to have risen to power in
the land of the Black City while it was in the hands of
foreign rulers (wrw and ḥk3w) squabbling among themselves.
He seems to have restored some order from the chaos
described as existing in the delta at that time but he
appears to have disregarded the Egyptians and the Egyptian
gods. Only later under Sethnakht and following him, Ramesses
III, was there the restoration of the rule of Egyptian law
and of the Egyptian gods. That is what the opening lines of
Plate 75 of the Papyrus Harris tell us. We hope to discuss
the concept of the Black Land, not as a name for Egypt, but
as an adjoining foreign territory, in a forthcoming study.

We have already emphasized that the sequence of
place-names and their relationship to each other which we
find in the ancient Egyptian contexts can carry no
enlightenment for us at present because none of those names
are scientifically and indisputably proved. It may now
happen that if our present identification of Irs is
accepted, as I believe it must, we may be able to identify
some of these other names by reference to Irs itself.

It is a pity that most of the Egyptian references to
Irs are in lists of countries which tell us nothing about it
in particular. One of these is from Medinet Habu, the
inscription of Year 8, that is, from the texts which have
always been associated with the so-called Sea Peoples. Since

1972,[126] I have been saying that these texts have not been even remotely understood by us because the interpretation of the references they contain was arbitrarily decided last century with the first reading of these texts, without the support of any scientific evidence for those identifications. To this day few scholars have troubled to reconsider them. It is, one must admit, a very difficult task to do this because the names are so closely linked to each other in the texts that it is difficult to consider them completely objectively. In the case of the Inscription of Year 8, the appearance of Irs in lines 16-17 must make us think again about the political relations of neighbouring states in ancient times. In the discussion on Wenamun, I considered another of the names which also occurs on this particular list, Ḵd. I argued then that it may logically be considered to lie where the Nile water turns around to flow in the opposite direction, between Lake Timsah and the Gulf of Suez (see our fig. 2). This country too is not so far from the Nile valley, if this identification is accepted. Yet this was clearly far enough for it to have been inhabited by foreigners who were sometimes hostile to the Pharaoh. Regrettably we do not yet have adequate studies of the names contained in these texts. What is most discouraging, however, is that the approach of scholars to them even today relies on the tentative identifications of the early Egyptologists. There is no truly critical approach which would require a radical reconsideration of all the

170

lists of foreigners and an admission that many of the names
explained for us until now are no more than proposals based
on assumptions and presented without evidence.

More than in any other Egyptian text, the Papyrus
Anastasi IV treats Irs as a close neighbour with which Egypt
had regular contacts and exchanged goods of everyday need.
None of the products of Irs mentioned there associate it
with Cyprus or any part of it, though Ricardo Caminos
accepted this idea without difficulty at the time he
published this translation.[127] Oils and cows have not been
particularly associated with Cyprus and it could not have
been a regular practice to move precious animals across
rough seas in the small vessels that were used in
Mediterranean at that time. Furthermore, Egypt had plenty of
cattle attested as early as the Old Kingdom and this
reference to cows from Irs, as well as the request for a
bull by the Alashiyan King in Amarna Letter no. 35, clearly
indicates some special breeding activity there. The
possibility must also be considered that we may be talking
here of the humped cattle which are portrayed in harness
pulling quarried blocks of stone early in the Eighteenth
Dynasty.[128] They must have been a special and valued breed,
but they are not often portrayed in the Egyptian reliefs.

As to the oils called dft and jnb in Papyrus Anastasi
IV, it is not unreasonable to suggest that they may be
products of certain cities within Irs. If it is true that

the country of Irs lay within the general area of Kharu, this would link up with the oil products listed elsewhere for this area,[129] chiefly as nḫḫ-oil, as we have already stated in our discussion of Kharu earlier. We could even suggest that the ḏft-oil mentioned in this text could be associated with the town called Dftj (perhaps named after that oil), which is listed in the first campaign of the Annals of Tuthmosis III.[130] If so, it could refer to a special product made perhaps from some locally-grown plant. Very possibly, this town could correspond to the one called Djiftah (Zifta) during the 10th and 12th centuries A.D. (see our fig. 5),[131] in the central delta, not far from the town called El ᶜAras.

This reference to the oil products of Irs may be linked to the request for some special oil by the King of Alashiya in Amarna Letter 35. Clearly the whole region was productive of oil of various kinds and each would have had its own special qualities. The study of the oils mentioned in the ancient Egyptian texts has only just begun in recent years,[132] and it will be some time before we shall be able to identify them with any certainty.

Scholars have made much of the reference in Papyrus Anastasi IV, 17:7 to the ḏhw-metal carried on the necks of the children of Irs. Mindful of the fact that the ancient texts generally refer to Irasa/Alashiya as a copper-producing country, for a closer look at this word, which has

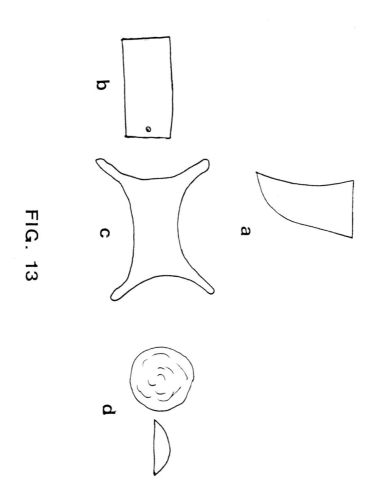

FIG. 13

been translated as <u>lead</u>[133] and <u>tin</u>, we need a brief parenthesis.

viii) <u>Some Relevant Remarks on the Egyptian Words for Copper</u>

It is significant that the ancient Egyptian word for copper, <u>bj3</u>, possibly a generic term for <u>metal</u> from the earliest times, actually means <u>separation</u> as early as the Old Kingdom.[133] This shows that the ancient Egyptians were always aware of the process by which the metal was extracted from the ore. It seems likely, however, that the raw material was processed near the mines and that only the separated metal was brought back to Egypt, probably in ingots, which we know to have had various shapes.[134] It is probable that this term <u>bj3</u> referred also to iron later on, though the expression known to us to refer to iron is <u>bj3 n pt</u>, <u>metal from the sky</u>, i.e. <u>meteoric iron</u>, which can be recognised as such by its physical structure, containing nickel.

The other Egyptian word which specifically means <u>copper</u> is <u>ḥmt</u>, written as the first sign in our fig. 13. It was mistakenly thought to be an ingot[135] and this belief still prevails today among some scholars even though no ingot of this shape has ever been known nor has it ever been suggested by any evidence at all. However, crucibles of this shape are often seen on the reliefs[136] and other vessels of this shape were used also in the copper-working process.

Papyrus Harris Plate 40 b:

12

6784

13

6784

14

6784

Papyrus Harris Plate 21 b:

14

112132

after Erichsen

FIG. 14

The ancient Egyptian texts use various qualifications with bj3 and ḥmt to describe the variety of metal they are referring to, but so far we have been unable to understand them and we have only been able to speculate upon these. However, the Papyrus Harris carries some clues for us which may profitably be examined here in order to understand the passage we have referred to above in Papyrus Anastasi IV.

One of these expressions has been ḥmt km which we have so far accepted as black copper, following Breasted's translation of the Papyrus Harris. Yet this expression conveys nothing to us. However there is another meaning for km which has until now been overlooked, namely completion.[137] It is possible to translate ḥmt km as completed copper, thus possibly bronze, though it is not clear from this term whether tin or arsenic has been added to harden it. This translation is more acceptable because it is more likely, particularly as another expression exists to confirm it.

Evidence that we may be right in accepting ḥmt km as completed copper may be found in another expression which has not been understood until now, namely ḥmt ᶜḥᶜ. Breasted translated this expression in the Papyrus Harris[138] as "raised" copper, but this expression also conveys nothing to us. However, ᶜḥᶜ may be accepted as meaning incomplete, so that ḥmt ᶜḥᶜ may well be referring to incomplete copper, meaning probably copper without the necessary additives to make it into bronze.

This proposal for a new, yet literal, translation of these two expressions opens up for us fresh possibilities for understanding these difficult texts. It also indirectly throws light on the word d̲ḥw which is used for the metal which the children from Irs were carrying on their shoulders as stated in Papyrus Anastasi IV, 17:7-8. The general acceptance by scholars of this term has been that it refers to tin or lead. Although some doubt was expressed by Egyptologists on these tentative identifications [139], non-Egyptologists have not been so cautious. All are aware of some blue-grey blocks (also called "slate-coloured") labelled with this name in the tomb of Rekhmire.[140] This colour is consistent with lead but not with tin, which is very light-coloured in its pure state.

The term d̲ḥw or d̲ḥ, d̲ḥj may be found by itself in a few texts, but not many, as J.R. Harris noted.[141] He believed, as did Caminos[142], that this term should be distinguished from d̲ḥtj. We might have taken the two terms to be synonymous had it not been that in the Papyrus Harris they occur together three times (see our fig. 14) thereby indicating some distinction between them.

The Papyrus Harris Plate 21b, line 14 shows[143] us three names grouped together as in our fig. 14 here:

ḥmt km, completed copper or bronze

ḥmt d̲ḥt, lead copper

d̲ḥw   ?   112132 objects in all.

Let us say at once that the interpretation of d̲h̲t as lead here is well supported because the same word with the same meaning is to be found in the later Coptic, whereas it is significant that a new word enters that language for tin as though there had been nothing there previously to satisfy that particular requirement. We may safely rule out the possibility that d̲h̲t here is referring to tin.

Furthermore, the reference to lead copper here is appropriate because this section of the Papyrus is listing statues of gods.

Paul Craddock has shown[144] that the addition of lead to copper lowers its viscosity and improves its casting properties for statues. However this variety of copper would not be suitable where a hard metal was required.

The third name on our list quoted above from the Papyrus Harris d̲h̲w (d̲h̲jjw) is unlikely to be referring to another metal. There are two other places in that Papyrus, namely in Plate 68 a, 1 and in Plate 40 b, 14, where d̲h̲w is listed after d̲h̲t, lead and it is shown at all times to be in the plural. It is therefore very likely that the third word on our list may be in apposition to the first two, as a summary of those. Thus it could read:

completed copper (bronze),

lead copper,

ingots (altogether) 112132.

This is likely because, as we see in fig. 14, only this last

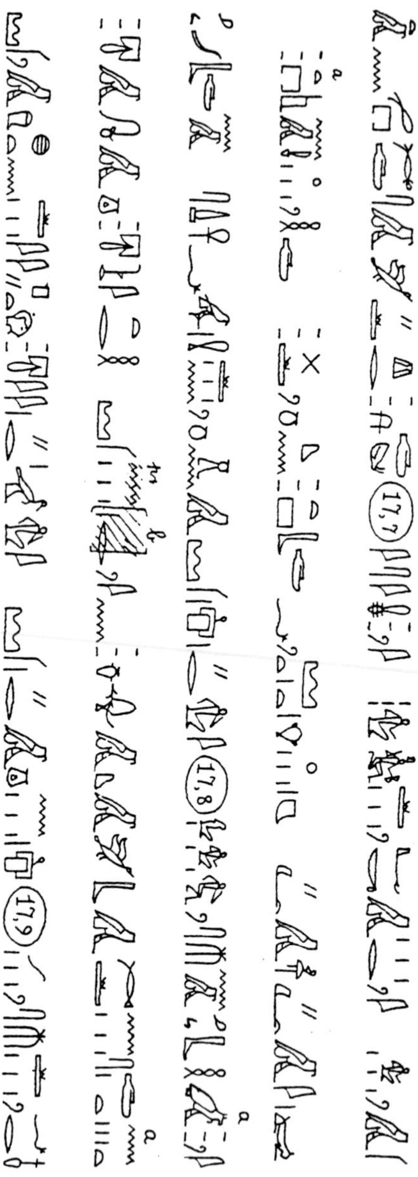

FIG. 15

after Gardiner

name carries the brick determinative. If we are right in this interpretation, then the Papyrus Anastasi IV text is telling us that the children of Irs were bringing dhw, meaning material delivered in a brick-shaped ingot, as well as material brought in another measure called nmswt.

The translation of the text of Papyrus Anastasi IV, 17:7-8 (fig. 15 here) by Ricardo Caminos is perhaps oversimplified and his note on this particular passage is not totally clear.[145] In the actual text we find:

copper from its hill-country, a common expression meaning presumably copper ore in the state in which it came out of the mountain;

dbwt knww, knww being probably the equivalent of knkn as in the Wörterbuch V, 55f, where an example quoted refers to copper, meaning bricks of broken-down or scrap metal.

dhw nmswt, for which Caminos rightly underlines the fact that nmst can refer to a unit of weight or measure. It is therefore not impossible that we may have here dhw meaning brick-shaped ingots and nmswt meaning another kind of measure of this same material.

I hope to be able to say more about this last name in a forthcoming study.

ix)   How this geographical identification fits in with the evidence from the Amarna Letters

The Amarna Letters are something of a phenomenon in that this cuneiform archive is the only one of its kind to

have been found in Egypt.[146] That is not to say that other
archives may not have existed or may still exist there. But
excavators in Egypt in the past have been so intent on
looking for inscribed blocks that they have not only not
recognized much of the evidence for foreign settlements in
Egypt, particularly in the delta. They have actively
destroyed it. With regard to the cuneiform tablets of the
Amarna archive, it is certainly true that unless the clay
had been fired or the tablets burned in a palace fire, it is
unlikely that they would have been preserved in Egypt in
recent years, when the water table had risen considerably,
especially in the delta. Furthermore it could be argued
that, in an agricultural environment, the cuneiform script
on clay could be mistaken for the imprint of hen's feet!

Most of Hellbing's study of Alashiya is devoted to a
detailed study of the content of the Amarna Letters[147] and
this is not surprising as they yield more information than
any other source we have so far. However, his dependence on
the text-book identification of the place-names involved in
this discussion did not help us to understand the problems
as we might have done otherwise.

I have already pointed out elsewhere[148] that the
names of the rulers of Gubla, Rid-addi and Ilirabih, which
we find in the Amarna Letters, are not otherwise attested
anywhere, not even in the monuments from Gebeil/Byblos. For
this and other reasons, we should consider the possibility

that the Gubla of the Amarna Letters may not be Gebeil/Byblos at all. I have suggested that the kbn/kpnj of the ancient Egyptian texts was probably El Gibali, situated on the south-west shore of Lake Timsah,[149] basing myself on the evidence alone, and we may well find that the eight Amarna Letters from Alashiya that we have may lead us, upon further reflection, to reconsider our proposals made so far in an effort to identify this country.

We have a basic geographical clue in Amarna Letter 114 in which we are told that the ruler of Gubla had sent an Egyptian official home through Alashiya. Thus this country was situated between Gubla and Egypt. We have already said elsewhere that Gubla could theoretically represent any place which was called Gebal in ancient times and we have emphasized that this was a very common name in the Near East[150]. If the Gubla of the Amarna Letters was the same place as the kbn/kpnj of the Egyptian texts, where Wenamun went to get his pine wood, it is quite possible that this may have been El Gibali, south-west of Lake Timsah, as we have already said. A route from El Gibali to Egypt, avoiding the Wadi Tumilat, would take a messenger through Alashiya as we have defined it here (see fig. 16.).

This area conforms with the requirements we infer from the Amarna Letters[151] that Alashiya was an independent country with its own ruler and had many cities within its territory. It is also very important to note that the

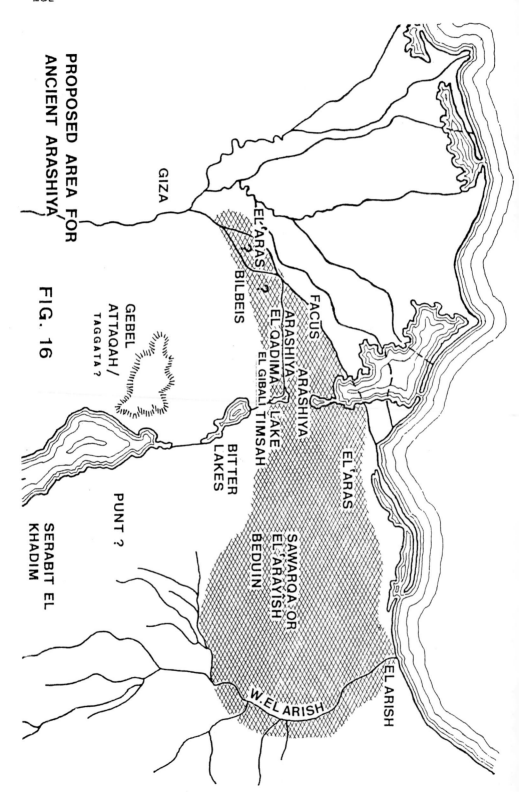

PROPOSED AREA FOR ANCIENT ARASHIYA

FIG. 16

GIZA

EL'ARAS ?

BILBEIS

FACUS

ARASHIYA

ARASHIYA EL QADIMA LAKE

EL GIBALI TIMSAH

EL 'ARAS

SAWARQA OR EL 'ARAYISH BEDUIN

GEBEL ATTAQAH /
TAGGATA ?

BITTER LAKES

PUNT ?

SERABIT EL KHADIM

W. EL ARISH

EL ARISH

territory of Alashiya had access to the sea at El Arish, as we know it today, while it also had a port on the north shore of Lake Timsah, which is still called Arashiya today. It is clear from the Letters that the relations between that country and Egypt go back at least a number of generations before the Amarna Period.

Scholars have made much of the fact that Alashiya was a producer of copper, which we discuss in a separate section here. But a particularly interesting fact about this country was that it was a source for timber. Letter 35, lines 27-29 tell us of the annoyance of the ruler of Alashiya because the Egyptians were taking wood from his territory without paying for it. Therefore this had to be a place where the timber could be taken by the ancient Egyptians without the certainty of being caught in the act. It may have been along a border territory. But this could certainly not have been carried out from the territory of another foreign country, however friendly to Egypt, because of the politically complicated repercussions following such events.

These facts fit in with the abundant evidence we have presented elsewhere[152] for the presence of timber in thick forests in southern Palestine and perhaps extending into the delta of Egypt from pre-biblical times until our own.

The production of timber as a primary industry of Alashiya also made it an important ship-building country. Amarna letter 36, line 13, tells us that it supplied vessels to Egypt, a country which depended heavily on water transport. But this does not necessarily mean the provision of sea-going vessels for Egypt. I have discussed elsewhere the total lack of evidence for sea-going on the part of the ancient Egyptians.[153] It seems that they did not need to go abroad because all the countries came to Egypt!

The ruler of Alashiya in Letter 35, line 4 assures the Pharaoh that his chief men, his horses and his chariots were all in good condition. The climate in Alashiya must also have been conducive to the breeding of horses as well as cattle, with no shortage of fodder and water. In our earlier section on Wenamun, we referred to the evidence for the movement of horses between Egypt and the lands of Kharu, implying the certainty that they would come to no harm along that route.

The political events reflected in the Amarna Letters with regard to Alashiya include the report of the attacks by the Lukki (one of the so-called Sea Peoples) who, the Alashiyan ruler complains, each year occupy a further small portion of his land. We find therefore that as early as the Amarna Period, there were attacks by invading groups in areas not very far from Egypt. The Pharaoh in fact accuses some people in Alashiya of having joined forces with the Lukki in order to attack the borders of Egypt. The Alashiyan ruler is at a loss for words as the result of the accusation, which means that it was probably quite true.

From this we see that Egypt was well within the range of marauding bands from Alasa and therefore this fits in well with our new geographical proposal for the identification of Alashiya.

Furthermore, Letter 35 reveals that the Alashiyan ruler was worried about any possible treaties between Egypt and the Hatti countries and Sanhar. Clearly his worry was that they might constitute an imminent threat to his country. It is not clear to us at present where exactly we should place Hatti and Sanhar. However, what is clear from this letter from Alashiya is that its ruler was keenly worried about the threat to his country which such treaties could pose. This implies an uncomfortable proximity.

Hellbing noted[154] that the ruler of Alashiya never asks Egypt for gold, but that the Letters request silver from Egypt. At present we know of no certain sources for silver in Egypt. Yet the repeated requests by the Alashiyan ruler for silver from Egypt make it certain that, during the Amarna period at any rate, Egypt was a producer of silver. So far, the galena deposits of Gebel Rosas and Gebel Zeit, along the Red Sea, have yielded only so-called "non-commercial" quantities of silver and the suggestion has been made that these sites were worked out in antiquity.

x)   How this identification fits in with the evidence from the non-Egyptian documents.

We do not propose here to discuss the textual

problems of the non-Egyptian texts relating to Alashiya nor the uncertainties concerning their date. We simply wish to see whether their general content appears to allow our identification of Alashiya, the place which still bears this name today and marked on our sketch map no. 5.

It seems that the earliest reference that we have to Alashiya is in a text on a tablet from Mari, found by Dossin[155] to which we referred in an early section of this discussion. This country is also mentioned from some as yet unpublished texts from that site.[156] However these references, like many other later ones, do not contain any clues that might help us identify Alashiya.

From Alalakh we have two texts mentioning this country with reference to grain and a payment of silver.[157] From a different level at this same location we have two tablets also mentioning Alashiya, but again without any important clues for its identification, beyond lists containing names.

We next find this name in the Ugaritic texts which name various countries and their inhabitants.[158] The names of men, women and children from Alashiya are listed here besides those of Hittite and Hurrite lands. Muhly describes UT 119 as some sort of census list[159] giving the names of women and children from "the town of Alashiya". Also "captive workers" are mentioned here in conjunction with "the town of Alashiya'. Muhly identifies as Hurrian some of the names that are stated to come from Alashiya in UT 119.[160] Other personal names in this text, he tells us, are Semitic and Anatolian (sic). Muhly concludes that the population of Alashiya was probably as ethnically mixed as that of Ugarit and that ties between Ugarit and Alashiya were strong.

We shall not here discuss the date of the "Madduwatta text", which seems to be the first Hittite document referring to Alashiya, the date of which may possibly be as early as 1400 B.C.[161]

The importance of the "Madduwatta Text" for us here lies in the fact that in it, the Hittite king claims sovereignty over Alashiya, rightly or wrongly.[162] Such a claim, whether true or false, must have been a possible one, at any rate, so that we must place Alashiya within range of the Hittite empire at this date (uncertain though it may be). We may well find that we must move the Hittites much further south for this period. It is, in any case, much more probable that the Hittites could claim sovereignty over Alashiya, as we are identifying it here, on the mainland, than over Cyprus or some part of it, across the sea.

Scholars have made much of the Hittite texts from the time of Suppliluliumas II, in which some battles on water are mentioned.[163] These have been interpreted as Sea Battles, though with considerable surprise on the part of scholars, because the Hittites are not known as a seafaring people.

I have it on good authority that there is no word for _sea_ in the Hittite language. In fact, even the word for _lake_ appears to be rather vague. Therefore it seems fair to say that there is no certainty that any Hittite battle took place on any sea, rather than on an inland water or a river. I cannot discuss this but merely mention it here in passing. However, it is immaterial for the sake of our argument whether the Hittites fought on the sea or on land. There is at least one seaport in the region we are identifying as Alashiya, namely at El Arish. From this port on the Mediterranean, any approaching foreign ships could presumably have been seen for some distance coming from the north, or the south or the west.

On the other hand, the present town of Ismailia is the site of an ancient port on a large expanse of inland water, which was once much larger than it is today and which is still called _Arashiya_ by the local population.

It is a regrettable fact that Egyptologists and some others are unwilling to accept the ancient world as a much more intimate one than is the case today. They are reluctant to consider battles between neighbouring cities and on inland waters. Their concept of a state is of a political region rather than of a mound/city with its own administration within its few acres.[164]

However, we have to admit that Alashiya appears to offer textual evidence that it is an exception to this rule, as we see by the extent of the area by which we are identifying it here. An explanation of this may lie in the meaning of the root of its name, if we are right in accepting its meaning as a tenting-place, originally.

As is to be expected, Hellbing and other scholars use the Sea Peoples so-called to explain the events in the Madduwatta text and in others.[165] Unfortunately he quotes Nancy Sandars as his sole authority on this even though all the texts dealing with these attacks are from Egyptian sources only. These are hardly touched upon in her book and are actually wrong in some important basic respects. One of these is her description of the Egyptian delta as flat.[166] This was untrue up to one hundred years ago, when the travellers described the hundreds of mounds that were to be seen at that time, most of which have today been destroyed by bulldozers, without record. An understanding of the history of the Egyptian delta, as well as its physical nature is essential to an undertanding of the attacks on Egypt in this area.

In emphasizing that the Egyptian texts are the only historical sources naming the so-called Sea Peoples,[167] we must also underline the fact that a great deal more has been read into these texts than the evidence will legitimately and scientifically allow.

Furthermore, until now neither Egyptologists nor others would take into account the undeniable fact that there was no example at all in the Egyptian texts where Great Green or ym could be proved to mean sea. Egyptologists have now begun to acknowledge that I have been right in saying this[168], because my opponents have been unable, since 1972, to produce a single example to prove me wrong. Thus the interpretation that Egypt's foreign attackers were from the sea is totally unfounded and therefore quite untenable.

I do not propose here to continue my own discussion of the so-called Sea Peoples. I soon realised with the help of the late Professor John Barns, who taught me the rudiments of Egyptian grammar and the hieroglyphs, that the many lacunae in our understanding of the geographical terms used in the ancient Egyptian texts would not allow us to make any progress in this respect until a great many of these names had been studied individually and in depth. This may not occur in our own lifetime because too many scholars have been well satisfied with the assumptions that were adopted last century and have felt no need to re-examine them. Alashiya is listed among these many names which we cannot yet identify scientifically[169] and satisfactorily.

The idea that Alashiya lay across the sea for the Hittites was encouraged by the clues which suggest that it was an island, to which the Hittites deported their criminals.[170] This may well have been the case. One of the texts[171] refers to the sending of political offenders "over the water" to Alashiya.

Olivier Masson in 1973[172] showed that one reference at least suggested that Alashiya may have been an island, which, he believes, proves conclusively that Alashiya was Cyprus. However, the first thing to be emphasized here was that this tablet or amulet was not found on Cyprus and therefore does not necessarily have anything to do with that island. The second thing to be emphasized is that this tablet was bought, not found on an archeological site. We are told that it was bought by R. du Mesnil du Buisson in 1933 but that it was not made available to scholars until 1972.[173] The text carries a spell against a demon and refers to "the man from the island of Alashiya".[174] This is quite likely to be fact, but not with reference to Cyprus.

We have already referred to the large area of swampland which surrounded Lake Timsah right up to the time of the cutting of the Suez Canal through this lake. This area of swampland is marked clearly on the Napoleonic Survey map for this area[175] and even later on the maps of the Geological Survey of Egypt, up to fifty years ago. It would have been perfectly normal for a mound representing a town to be surrounded by water during the annual inundation, but in this area the water remained more than anywhere else in the delta, because it is, around Lake Timsah, at its lowest level. This would result in the thickest and most enduring swampland in the delta, which would also have been a breeding ground for crocodiles as the name of Timsah, t3 msḥ tells us. Thus it may well have been true that the town of Alashiya, situated on the present site of Ismailia, which is still called by this name by the local inhabitants today, may well have in earlier times been an island in the middle of one of the densest swamplands in the delta, infested by crocodiles. This would have been an ideal place for the holding of political prisoners.

I said earlier that there are many aspects of the non-Egyptian texts referring to Alashiya over which I have no control and therefore am unable to discuss. What I should like to see is a Hittite specialist studying this new identification for Alashiya with reference to the other names mentioned with it.

xi)   Gebel Attaqah as a Source for Copper and Possibly as the Mount Taggata of the Hittite Texts

Gebel Attaqah (variously written Ataqa, Attaka, Ataka etc.) is the highest mountain in Egypt. It rises massively west of Suez and extends for many miles in the direction of Cairo. Overlooking as it does the northernmost part of the Gulf of Suez, it also dominates the city of Suez. This was in ancient times a junction point for several trade routes and a transit area for foreigners. Though not very close to the Nile, it was close enough for ancient Egypt to have known of their presence and to have kept alert to this threat. The Napoleonic Survey in the early nineteenth century calls this mountain El Taqa. We must note that this name is not unique, though not common. At least one other mountain of this name is known from the Sudan.

This mountain has never been completely surveyed,[176] not only because of its vastness and physically difficult terrain. Its location is in an area where hostilities have occurred in the recent past, so that the remains of military installations are a real obstacle to the carrying out of archeological surveys.

Local rumor has it that some giant figures are carved in the rock somewhere or other on Gebel Attaqah. But the fact is that this mountain has been heavily quarried for many centuries, with ever increasing intensity in our own times. No-one has ever looked to see whether any ancient inscriptions are left on its surface, before being crushed into filling for the cement of Cairo.

Among the few early travellers who left an account of their visit to this mountain was Jacques Daumas who was there in 1948.[177] He gave its height as 871 metres at its highest point. He noted that this mountain consisted of a plateau surrounded by cliffs stretching towards the east. Many wadis were created by this mountain which can today best be seen on satellite photographs. The very rugged nature of this mountain and its dangers if explored without a suitable guide were emphasized by Jean-Edouard Goby as a result of his visit in 1939-42.[178]

All the way up the mountain face which can be seen from the road along the Gulf of Suez there are many holes, which could be entrances to caves or possibly to ancient mines. Jacques Daumas noted the remains of some ancient buildings at the top of the plateau, including a stone circle which he thought might have been used as a well to conserve water. We should not exclude the possibility that this may have been a habitation structure similar in shape to the nawamis found by Petrie and others in the Sinai. Heaps of flints were found in considerable number near the old buildings. These are particularly significant as Mount Attaqah itself has no sources of this material which means it must have been brought there to set up a workshop of some kind. In one of the caves to the north of these ruins Daumas found clear signs of habitation.[179] Moreover, nearby above the Wadi Um Reseis, he found some low walls which he describes as shepherd's huts.[180] There was also a cistern of 4-5 metres for the conservation of water after rain.

It is also significant that on top of the plateau near the ruins Daumas found large quantities of snail shells, some clearly more recent than others, without any indication as to their possible date.[181] He also noted that there were no living snails in the area when he was there.

Gebel Attaqah consists chiefly of limestone and dolomite. The geological studies of this mountain have been fragmentary so far, though a completely up-to-date study of its physical structure is now under way by the Geological Survey of Egypt and Mines Department.

I first applied to the Department of Egyptian Antiquities to carry out a general archaeological survey of the area north and north-east of the mountain in 1979, and I was asked to supply more details, which I did, re-applying in 1980. Our purpose was precisely to look for inscriptions on the eastern and northern faces of the mountain as systematically and as far as we could, plotting the area covered on to a map. Furthermore our purpose was to look for surface signs of ancient metal-working on Gebel Attaqah. We had in our team scientists with experience of this on the Greek mainland, as well as of technical knowledge of the metal itself. The authorities were worried about the security aspect of the project, but further assurances were given. In January 1981, permission was given for the project by the Executive Committee of the Egyptian Antiquities Department. However, we were never allowed to begin work even though we had completed all the arrangements and had the full support of the Suez Governorate, as well as of the security authorities.

The special importance of this mountain may be seen in a text from the end of the reign of Ramesses III, the Papyrus Harris.[182] It speaks of an expedition to a place called Atika for the purpose of obtaining bj3, copper.[183] It is the only pharaonic reference we have so far to a place of this exact name and scholars have suggested that, as the text refers to copper (or possibly to any metal which was separated from the ore), it had to refer to one of the places which we already know to have produced copper in ancient times. I suggested in 1975 that the Atika of this text must be our Gebel Attaqah, not only because its name is still identical. Linguists know that place names change very little over the centuries because they are not of everyday use. But there are other reasons for my suggestion that Gebel Attaqah is the Atika of the Papyrus Harris.

James Breasted translated[184] this particular section of the papyrus (Plate 78, lines 1 ff) as follows:
"I sent forth my messengers to the country of Atika, to the great copper mines which are in this place. Their galleys (mnš vessels) carried them (were laden with them); others on the land journey were upon their asses. It has not been heard before since the reign (of kings began). Their mines were found abounding in copper; it was loaded by ten-thousands into their galleys. They were sent forward to Egypt (to the Black City) and arrived safely. It was carried and made into a heap under the balcony (of the palace) in many bars (bricks) of copper, like hundred-thousands, being of the colour of gold of three times (three times as brilliant as gold). I allowed all the people to see them like wonders."
Here it is clearly the pharaoh Ramesses III who is speaking. The preceding passage in this text refers to the Punt

expedition[185] while the following passage refers to the turquoise country, mfkt, which Breasted, erroneously as we know now, translated as malachite. We know this turquoise country to have been Serabit El Khadim and Maghara in the Sinai (see fig. 5). It is significant that Atika is mentioned in this text between Punt and the turquoise-producing country which we know to have been in the Sinai. A glance at our sketch map fig. 5 will show that our proposals for these areas make them neighbours and therefore acceptable as a logical sequence of names as they are presented to us in the historical section of the Papyrus Harris.

This text makes it clear that Atika could be reached both by land and water which agrees with our emphasis on the importance of the Wadi Tumilat since 1975.[186] It is a great pity after all our efforts that we are still unable to say where the ancient copper mines were situated on Gebel Attaqah, as well as living in the knowledge that any surface inscriptions on this mountain are being destroyed. We have already said that this mountain is composed of limestone and dolomite. Geologists admit that it is quite possible for copper to be present in some of the folds of this mountain. It would be encouraging to know that some rescue work was being done in this area, if all the ancient traces are not already obliterated by the many hundreds of quarries which are operating there today as also by the blasting operations of other projects which have already changed the historical outline of this mountain against the sky.

We have already referred to the variations in the writing of the name of Attaqah, including El Taqa as we find it in the Description de l'Egypte.[187]

The possibility should be considered that the mountain called Taqqata in the Hittite texts may well be the same mountain the name itself having undergone the process of metathesis. Like Attaqah, Taqqata is stated in the ancient texts to be a good source of copper. Gerd Steiner in 1962 published a text[188] which was a ritual for the erection of a temple which speaks of copper and bronze (sic) from the mountain Taqqata in Alashiya. Although Attaqah cannot be said to be situated literally within the area which we should define as Alashiya at present, because we would at present confine Alashiya to the area of lowland and dunes mainly along the northern coast, nevertheless Attaqah is an imposing presence in that whole area and might well justify the statement that it lay in Alashiya for that very reason. Alternatively, we may find upon further study that the Attaqah area may have to be included within the region of ancient Alashiya. For the present, however, we must confine ourselves to the area further north, where the remaining place-names from this root indicate the probability that they were part of this region in earlier times.

In his discussion of Alashiya, James Muhly referred[189] to some unpublished texts from Mari found by

Dossin which speak of copper "from the mountain of Alashiya", as though there was only one mountain worth considering as such in Alashiya. These appear to date from the first half of the eighteenth century B.C. It is possible that these texts are referring to Taqqata, possibly our Attaqah. But we must not exclude the other possibility that the mountain of Alashiya may be the extensive highland in the centre of the Sinai, through which the Wadi Arish flowed and gathered water before it reached the town of El Arish on the Mediterranean Sea (see our fig. 5).

We shall return below to other sources of copper in these regions as also to sources of gold, which the Alashiya texts tell us was so plentiful in that region.

xii)   Copper and Gold from Alashiya

The texts relating to Alashiya often mention copper and sometimes gold as a product of that country, as well as making some rare references to oils, lead and cattle from that country.

In one document from Boğazköy, gold is demanded by the Hittites as the principle tribute from Alashiya, copper assuming a second place.[190] Another document KBo 1 26 (CTH 216)[191] is a fragment of an Akkadian letter deriving from Boğazköy which seems to be asking the ruler of Alashiya for gold and objects of gold in considerable quantity. It seems to be a reminder that goods previously promised had not yet been delivered.[192] A cuneiform tablet of unknown

200

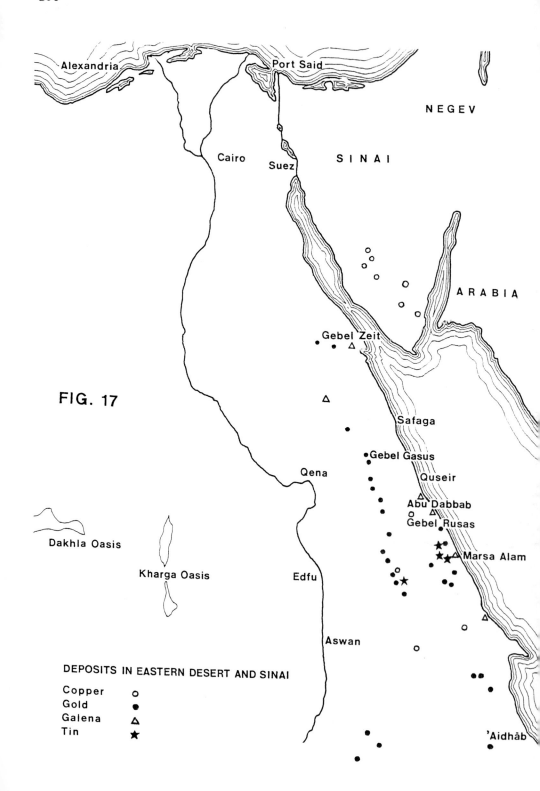

FIG. 17

DEPOSITS IN EASTERN DESERT AND SINAI

Copper ○
Gold ●
Galena △
Tin ★

provenance[193] now numbered WHM 114046 carries on its obverse side a long list of gold solar-discs and their weight and lists finally two items of bronze, possibly rings and vessels, ending with a reference to refined copper of Alashiya and Tilmun. It is not impossible that all the objects listed above the names of Alashiya and Tilmun should be understood as coming from those two sites.

We may just mention here in passing that Tilmun has been related to Punt by some scholars. The Egyptian monuments are quite explicit about copper and gold from Punt, as well as precious stones.[194] I have discussed this in considerable detail elsewhere and shall not repeat myself here,[195] though I would emphasize that all the evidence suggested placing Punt in the central, western Sinai as we show on our fig. 5 in this volume. We can see that Alashiya and Punt, as we define them from the evidence available are not very far from each other. We still have the problem, however, that geologists have not yet found gold in the Sinai. But that is not to say that it may not be present there.

The archaeological survey of the sites of the northern Sinai in 1973 [196] showed El Arish and another area near it to have yielded pieces of copper ore as well as implements such as needles and bodkins, which may be paralleled in some First Dynasty graves in Egypt.[197] It was noted early by J. Černý [198] and confirmed in recent years by

Beit Arieh and others[199] that the rarity of Egyptian pottery
in the Early Bronze Age II metal-working sites in southern
Sinai (see our fig. 17) suggested that the founders of
dynastic Egypt had no direct access to the copper mines
there. It must also be said that so far no intensive
clusters of hieroglyphic texts have been found on the walls
of those mountains, unlike the areas in the western central
Sinai at Serabit El Khadim and Maghara[200] and also at Timna
to a lesser extent.[201]

If we accept that Irs/Arasa/Alashiya was situated in
the area between Lake Timsah and the northern coastline as
far as El Arish, where did it get its copper and gold as the
texts affirm?

It has long been known that the Sinai had rich
sources of copper, particularly in the south and in recent
years these have been examined more closely[202] confirming
that they were exploited in ancient times. So far, however,
neither silver nor gold has been found in the Sinai in spite
of the fact that the Egyptian texts from Serabit El Khadim
and Maghara suggest that this did occur in pharaonic times.

It is quite possible that Alashiya may have received
some of its copper and its gold from the Eastern Desert,
which now belongs to Egypt, but which in ancient times was a
land foreign to the dweller along the Nile. There is no
doubt that the Eastern Desert was not part of Egypt during
Pharaonic times. Here too there are very few places where

the ancient Egyptians left evidence of their presence by means of hieroglyphic inscriptions on the walls of the mountains, as they did, quite exceptionally, in the quarrying area of the Wadi Hammamat.[203] The Egyptian records show that it was not until the Middle Kingdom that some Egyptian adventurer/explorers were sent systematically into these foreign areas to discover possible new sources of wealth for the Pharaoh.[204]

It is important to emphasize that we still do not have a final and irrevocable picture of the content of the mountains in the northern Eastern Desert and of Gebel Attaqah as a whole. We cannot therefore be dogmatic about the sources of copper and gold in that area at the present time, either separately or together.

The Eastern Desert has yielded copper and gold together on several sites (see our fig. 17 here) and often in rich quantities as at Hammash[205].

The mediaeval Arab writers refer constantly to the area of the Wadi El Allaki, south-east of Aswan, as an area abounding in gold and silver mines, which was in the hands of the Beja tribes. Near this area was also the emerald mine, well-known for its excellent gems.[206] Some of the writers speak of the mountains in this area while others describe it as a flat area, clearly referring to the wadi itself. But the facts generally recorded are indisputable: Wadi El Allaki was renowned for its gold and its silver and

FIG. 18 a

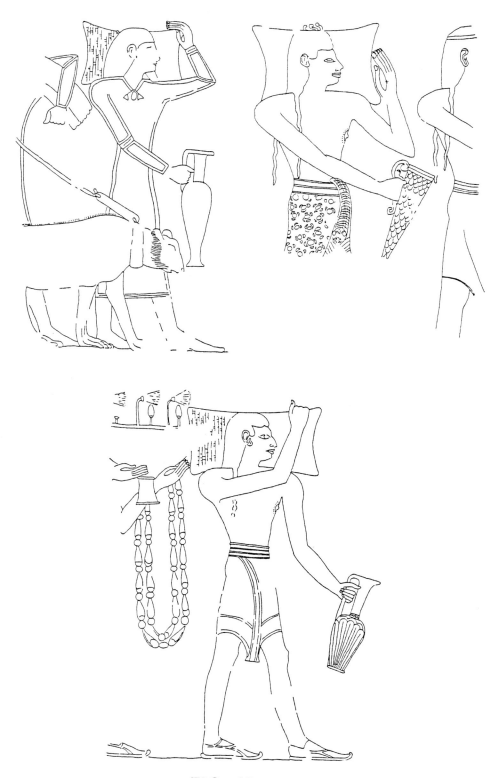

FIG. 18 b

in some places, yielded gold "unmixed with silver" [207]. This confirms for us the usual source of the silver as it must have been even in mediaeval times, namely, the abundant gold of the mines of the eastern desert.

xiii) A brief note on Egypian silver

The most recent and complete review and study of Egyptian sources of silver and its use is in the article "Ancient Egyptian Silver" by N.H. Gale and Z.A. Stos-Gale in JEA 67 (1981), 103-115. This followed their study of sources of galena, lead and silver in predynastic Egypt in Revue d'Archéometrie 6 (1980) and many other aspects of this problem are treated in other articles.[208] Their work is based on direct analysis of the ancient objects and sets out to test previous theories and preliminary results by pioneers such as Alfred Lucas, who had led the way remarkably accurately, as it turns out.

As far back as 1928, Alfred Lucas had produced tables showing the results of his analyses of objects of ancient Egyptian gold, electrum and silver[209]. He found the gold objects to contain from 72 to 96 per cent of gold and from 3 to 18 per cent of silver, with occasionally a little copper. The electrum he found to be essentially an alloy of gold and silver containing approximately from 60 to 80 per cent gold and from 20 to 30 per cent of silver, with occasionally a little copper. As to the silver, he found this also to be an alloy of gold and silver containing approximately from 3 to

38 per cent of gold and from 60 to 92 per cent of silver, with occasionally a little copper. Thus all three were varieties of the same alloy and only differed in the relative proportions of the principal constituents.

At that time Alfred Lucas pointed out that it was not generally taken into account by metallurgists working on Egyptian objects that an alloy of gold and silver, containing so large a proportion of silver as to have a white colour, was still to be found in Egypt in his own day. While this today would be classed as a poor quality of gold, in ancient times, when silver was a great deal more valuable than gold, this would have been treasured and such a source worked diligently. Lucas found early silver objects from Egypt to have flecks of gold in them. Lucas believed that the silver used in ancient Egypt in the earliest period did not come from argentiferous galena or other ores. These came into use only in comparatively late times.

The work of Noel Gale and Zophie Stos-Gale re-examined this whole question in greater depth and gave a much firmer scientific foundation to the early work of Alfred Lucas by numerous analyses of well-documented objects and a careful assessment of their results. They do not contradict Lucas, but open up a vaster horizon for sources of Egyptian silver besides the alluvial gold of the wadis, suggesting the possibility of imported silver. Further work will no doubt increase our understanding of this problem.

W.F. Hume wrote in 1937 in his Geology of Egypt Vol. 2, Part III, 778f that analyses of Egyptian gold had indicated that it contained a considerable amount of silver, the percentage being more or less constant for the same mine, but varying between different mines. It was particularly noted that, on the whole, the percentage of silver to gold is higher in the mountain mines of the eastern desert than in the mountains of the south.

It is unlikely that these mines in the eastern desert would have come under the direct jurisdiction of the pharaoh. However, these must have been more accessible to ancient Egypt, during the Amarna period at any rate, than to Alashiya, whose ruler had to beg for silver from the pharaoh, in several passages of his letters.

Attention has been drawn to the mediaeval Arab writers who told us about the sources of "pure gold, unmixed with silver", mainly from the Wadi El Allaki, implying that most of the gold found contained a considerable percentage of silver. Al Idrisi tells us that this mining area was situated at about 15 days' distance from Aswan in a northeasterly (sic) direction and lay within Beja territory. He tells us: "No moslem country is adjoining the town of Aswan on the eastern side except Jabal al-^{C}Allaqi, which is a mountain, the lower part of which consists of a dry wadi, where no water flows; but, if one digs in its bed, water is found at a shallow depth, gushing out abundantly. On this mountain there is the gold and silver mine, where scores of men searching for these metals (ma^{c}ādin) gather. Near Aswan on the southern side of the Nile there is a mountain, on the foot of which there is the emerald mine, in a desert region far from any village." [210]

The writer Al Istakhri (932-950 A.D.) wrote that this mine region was situated at about ten days' journey from the fortress on the Red Sea called Aydhab.[211] The writer Ibn Hawqal who wrote before 988 A.D. speaks of the area between Aswan and the Red Sea as inhabited deserts where gold mines are found. He describes El Allaki as a place in a flat, sandy plain broken only by a few hills and it was a mine of pure gold, without mixture of silver, he says. [212]

The writer Al Bakri (1028-1094 A.D.) also speaks of the El Allaki mines which were rich in silver and gold. They were situated along an eighteen-day route from Aydhab to Aswan. The frequent references to this route inland from the Red Sea means that travellers came from over the Red Sea to work at these mines or to buy the gold and the silver.[213]

But it was the writer from Baghdad called Al Mas^{c}udi who died in 956 A.D. who gives us the most interesting information of all in this respect, namely a version of the recipe for extracting silver from the gold. Speaking of the Nubians he says:

"Their countries are hot, scorched and black because of the drought and the predominating

power of the fiery element. In their country,
silver changes into gold: in other words,
this metal is (so) heated (tabkh) by the dry
heat and warmth of the sun that it becomes
gold. In fact, if such leaves of gold as are
extracted from the mine in a very pure state
are put on the fire with a mixture of salt
(milh) and ferrous sulphate (zāj) and bricks
(tūb) one would obtain the quintessence of
silver (fiddah khālisa baydā)." (Pellat II,
378). [214]

It is very probable that the great value of silver in
the ancient world was due to the fact that most of it had
to be extracted from the gold and that it was for this
reason more expensive to procure.

Furthermore one report speaks of taxes to be paid to
the sovereign on the gold extracted from the mines in the
Beja lands: [215] "They have a share in the profit of those
who work in them and pay to the agents of the Sultan in
Egypt, every year, 400 mithqal of gold from their mines
before it is melted and purified". In the course of time,
the payment of the tribute ceased and the Sultan was very
angry at collecting only one fifth of the gold, silver and
precious stones from these mines. The story of these events
is recorded and may be found, with bibliography, among G.
Vantini's translated passages.[216] While the detail of these
struggles for the control of the wealth extracted from these
mines is beyond our scope here, it is important to underline
the fact that the mines were held secure from intruding
groups by organized forces, which would have to be defeated
before power could be assumed by others.

It is very likely that mining activity during

pharaonic times was not very different from the way it went on during the early mediaeval period. The importance of regular supplies of food and water would have been the same and any irregularities in this respect could have been disastrous for the mine and its managing tribe as we are told by some of the early Arab writers (e.g. Vantini, cit. 105ff).

Thus we find that our early mediaeval texts confirm the fact that silver was derived from the gold and that people travelled from Arabia across the Red Sea to come to these mines in the Eastern Desert of Egypt to acquire the noble metals. There could also be local disturbances and pitched battles on these sites if one group attempted to overpower another which was in charge of the mine.

xiv)   The clay structure of the Alashiya tablets

From the earliest studies of the Alashiya tablets found at Tell Amarna in Egypt, scholars have wondered whether it might be possible to determine their physical provenance by means of an identification of the clay. Most recently, Lennart Hellbing re-examined their outward physical appearance and found six of them to be grey, one red-brown and another, red-yellow externally and yellow at the core.[217] All the tablets, he found, had surface polish and only two contain any grit in the clay.[218] Earlier attempts at such a study by Knudtzon did not bring forward any results.

In recent years, attempts have been made to examine clay from archaeological sites by various methods in some scientific detail, among them, the method of neutron activation analysis, which was used on the Alashiya tablets. The efforts by scientists to match particular ancient clays to known clay sources today have not been very successful so far but they are undoubtedly helpful and in time we may be able to refer to a comprehensive chart of the nature of the clays used in the ancient world.

With regard to the Alashiya tablets we have one study by Artzy, Asaro and Perlman[219] of two Amarna tablets now in the British Museum. They are numbered 29788 and 29789, are both written in cuneiform Akkadian and both contain the title of the King of Alashiya. The method used was neutron activation analysis and the two tablets were found to have a very similar chemical composition pattern, closer than is often the case with pottery groups.

Their study of 30 Late Bronze sherds from Enkomi as well as others from neighbouring areas showed that among the many sources of similar clays used there for pottery making, none of them were used to make the Amarna tablets. Sherd samples were studied from Kalopsidha, Kition, Kouklia and other coastal sites and it was found that none of the chemical composition patterns from these sites is close to that of the Amarna Letters.

These investigators also considered the question as

to whether these Amarna tablets might not be copies for the
archives rather than the original letters themselves. They
therefore compared them with various clays from Egypt, from
various sites. Although these Egyptian clays did not match
each other chemically, the similarity in pattern of the clay
is clear. The Alashiya tablets do not match this pattern.

The two Amarna tablets were found to be quite
different from all the Egyptian pottery that was analyzed by
this method. Nor can they be matched to any clay from
eastern Cyprus, though there was a chemical similarity
between these tablets and a group of Mycenaean III C 1
sherds from Kouklia. At that time these investigators
suggested further sampling and analyses from Cyprus and
North Syria until the correct matching was found.

It will now be very interesting to see whether the
clays from the north shore of Lake Timsah will satisfy the
requirements of these analyses as well as the other cities
called today El Arish and El ^{C}Aras (the one along the coast
as well as the one west of Bilbeis, all on our fig. 5 here),
as well as the greater area which have tentatively
defined as Alashiya on our map fig. 16. Nor should we
exclude the possibility of clays having been collected from
the extensive region of the Wadi El Arish (fig. 5).

We should recall here that in his study of the
southern Sinai[220] Itzhak Beit-Arieh found very strong, and
in some respects, unique links between that area and Arad.

Petrographical analyses of pottery samples revealed uniform qualities in several groups from Arad and from south Sinai, indicating that the clay source for the very common cooking pots at Arad I-III is the granite area of central, southern Sinai.

It will be interesting to discover what the scientific evidence will be after examination of these new clay sources.

xv) <u>Lapis Lazuli from Isj/Asj/Asija, probably a close neighbour of Irasa/Alashiya</u>

Lapis lazuli is such a rare product from any country that the very fact that we are told that it was mined at a particular place should help us to identify it. However, our physical and geological knowledge of many areas is still incomplete so that we cannot yet be helped by the availability of such information.

Considerable work has been done in recent years on this material from the archaeological point of view and it has been brought together for us by P. R. S. Moorey and Georgina Herrmann in an entry for the <u>Reallexikon für Assyriologie</u>.[221]

Although lapis lazuli was used very widely in the Near East and in Egypt during pharaonic times and earlier[222], so far, the only certain provenance for this stone known to us is the district of Keramo-Munjan in Badakshan[223]. However, the references to this stone, <u>ḫsbd</u>, in the Sinai Inscriptions not only mention it together with turquoise (mfkt) and other valuable stones from those mountains. Sometimes, the list of these precious goods follows the statement: "....they brought away every good product of this foreign land....". Furthermore, we often find the suggestion in these texts that the goddess Hathor keeps these precious materials concealed and reveals them only as a special favour to the particular pharaoh ruling at the time of that expedition.

I have already referred elsewhere[224] to the particular significance of Sinai Inscription 102 (Plate XVIV from the time of the Ammenemes III), on which two titles of the goddess Hathor are inscribed on either side of the head of the monument: the lady (or protectress) of mfkt, turquoise; the lady (or protectress) of hsbd, lapis lazuli. Hathor is an Egyptian goddess, never found by that name in any non-Egyptian context. Furthermore she is a patroness of the region of the pink mountains and the marshes which bordered upon Egypt's boundaries.

It is therefore clearly implied in these texts that hsbd was a local product. Unfortunately, no lapis lazuli has yet been found in the Sinai and geologists from the Egyptian Geological Survey and Mining Authority have told me that two surveys are at present under way in these areas and that they will bear in mind the texts of their forefathers to find out whether lapis lazuli is present there. We must add that they are not very hopeful of doing so. But the Egyptian texts from the Sinai do seem to suggest a local provenance for this stone.

When the Egyptian texts speak of ḥsbd, lapis lazuli from the country of Isj/Asj, which seems to have been a very close neighbour of Irasa/Alashiya, they may well have been referring to the Sinai. We have already shown in the early part of this study that there is no evidence which will allow us to accept Isj/Asj as another name for Irasa/Alashiya. In fact, the evidence indicates otherwise, because the two names appear together on several lists. It is not impossible that the name of Isj/Asj may have been the precursor of the name of Asia, as has been suggested, but there is no evidence for this. This would be interesting because it could be taken as a general name for the Sinai, particularly if we bear in mind the mediaeval writers who tell us that the Nile separated Africa from Asia. We know that the Romans accepted that Syria (and Phoenicia) began at Pelusium.

Be that as it may, when Moorey and Herrmann suggest that the Sinai may have been no more than a trading post for lapis lazuli, they may conceivably be right.[225] The inscriptions of the Sinai indicate two kinds of lapis lazuli: one is qualified by tfrrt, with the determinative for substance or grains; the other is qualified by stt (usually translated as Asiatic, but wrongly, I believe) with

the determinative of island. It must be acknowledged that
both kinds could be imported stone. From my own
observations I have concluded that stt is more likely to
mean imported.[226] However, since we find some people bearing
this name in the Egyptian texts, we have to accept that they
had a homeland somewhere. Both of these terms will be re-
examined in due course.

We must turn elsewhere for a possible source of lapis
lazuli, namely to the western desert and upper Egypt. The
Arab scholar Al Idrisi who wrote before 1170 A.D. said:[227]

> "In the Kharga Oasis there is the Jabal
> cAlsani, a very high mountain, the width of
> which at the foot is the same as that at the
> top. In this mountain there is a mine of
> lapis lazuli (hajar al-lazurd) which is taken
> to Misr for cutting......"

I have asked some scientific investigators to look
for this mine, but so far, no results can be reported.
Clearly this reference from Al Idrisi is to a stone and not
to be a blue colouring material, which has been suggested as
a possible meaning for hsbd.

Similarly, we are fortunate in having a very precise
description of lapis lazuli as a stone that was produced,
among many others, in Egypt, from Edward Brown in 1739:[228]
"There is also a blue Stone of great Beauty, which differs
from the Turquoise as well as from the Sapphire, being
opaque like the former, but in Colour inclining to the
latter; curiously sprinkled as it were with Grains of Gold".

Unfortunately he gives us no provenance for this.

The Egyptian Wörterbuch III, 334 quotes a relief from Philae in which a procession of Nubian nomes are shown to be bringing gifts and among them, Meroe is carrying lapis lazuli.[229] That is undoubtedly an important presentation of this problem, even though Meroe is situated beyond the boundaries of Egypt proper, very far south.

In the Coffin Texts, we find a reference to lapis lazuli of the Blue Land in Spell 594. It is listed with myrrh from the land of the god, costly stones from the isles and turquoise etc.[230] But this too does not give us a precise reference as to its origin.

The most precise reference that we have so far is that this valuable stone came from the Gebel ᶜAlsani in the Kharga Oasis. It is interesting to note that between the Kharga and the Dakhla oases there is a very broad limestone plateau which extends for almost the whole 200 kilometres or so which separates them. It is therefore not impossible that, if the limestone structure is such that it will allow for one mine of lapis lazuli at Kharga Oasis, there may be other concentrations of this stone at other sites, not far from there. Clearly this site was known to the mediaeval writers.

In this respect it is worth looking at a Hittite text of a ritual for the founding of a temple.[231] Line 36 of this text tells us that the lapis lazuli used in the construction of this temple had come from the highland of Dagnijara, while three lines further on, 39-40, we are told that the copper had come from Alashiya, from its highland Daggata (Taggata, Attaqah ?). I believe that Dagnijara could conceivably be a version of Dakhla, astonishing though it may be that such a name should have been known to the Hittites. Yet considering their association with Alashiya, we must consider them as having had closer physical connections with the Nile than we have thought until now. We must accept the fact that Kharga and Dakhla are sufficiently near to each other to be thought of as one extended unit in the middle of such a vast area of desert. This is all the more likely to have been accepted by people who did not know these areas at first hand.

xvi)   Conclusion

The long discussion attempting to identify Irs/Alasa/Alashiya has been based on little or no evidence and we must praise those scholars who adhered to the rational view that unless some evidence was forthcoming, it could not be said that Alashiya was Cyprus or a part of it. Having reviewed all the discussion, we found that little progress was possible because it was based on insecure foundations.

It is important to understand that Isj/Asj/Asija cannot be equated with Irs/Arasa/Alashiya, though they were probably neighbouring territories. Both names appear in at least two lists of countries, indicating clearly that they were not both referring to the same place. Furthermore a careful examination of the products of these two countries show that a distinction must be made between them, particularly as one of them produces lapis lazuli whereas the other does not.

We have established that a homogeneous geographical area involving several variations of the name of Irs/Arasa/Alashiya still exists today, not only with regard to the names of places but also with regard to the name of the people who inhabit the northern part of the Sinai peninsula. The name of Irs itself and its variations may be related to the Berber root meaning a tenting-place, which would be apt if we consider that the area seems to embrace the flat northern part of the peninsula.

We have looked at the way in which the various literary references fit in with our new proposed identification and I believe that the picture is an acceptable one, though much still remains to be discussed.

xvii)   A chronological bibliography of the discussion on
        this topic

1866   F. Chabas, Voyage d'un égyptien, 225f

1888   A.H. Sayce, "Babylonian Tablets from Tel el-Amarna".
        PSBA 10, 488-525.

1888   E. A. Wallis Budge, "On Cuneiform Despatches", PSBA
        10, 540-569 and Plates VIII and XI.

1888   G. Maspéro, "Le pays d'Alasia", Recueil de Travaux
        10, 209f

1889   H. Winckler, "Verzeichnis der aus dem Funde von El
        Amarna herrührendon Thontafeln", ZAS 27, 42-64,
        particularly 63f.

1889-   H. Winckler, Der Thontafelfund von El-Amarna, I-III.
1890

1893   W. Max Müller, Asien und Europa, pp. 261, 292, 394.

1894   C. Niebuhr, Studien und Bemerkungen zur Geschichte
        des alten Orients I, 97-102.

1895   C. Niebuhr, "Das Land Alasia", Zeitschrift für
        Assyriologie X, 257-264.

1897   W. von Bissing, Die Statistische Tafel von Karnak,
        47f.

1898   G. Maspéro, "La correspondence d'Amarna", Journal des
        Savants.

1906   R. von Lichtenberg, "Beiträge zur ältesten Geschichte
        von Kypros", MVAG 11, 1-15.

1913   H. R. Hall, "The Land of Alashiya", Journal of the
        Manchester Oriental Society, 36f.

1915   G. Maspéro, Popular Stories of Ancient Egypt,
        280-295.

1915   J.A. Knudtzon, Die El-Amarna-Tafeln.

1915   G.A. Wainwright, "Alashia-Alasa; and Asy", Klio
        14, 1-36.

1915   T. Smolenski, Ann. Serv. 15, 60f.

1921   F. Schachermeyer, "Zum ältesten Namen von Kyprus",
        Klio 17, 230-239.

1922   A. R. Hall, "The Peoples of the Sea", <u>Etudes Champollion</u>, 315f.

1922   G. Jéquier, <u>BIFAO</u> 19, 22f.

1925   H. Gauthier, <u>Dictionnaire des noms géographiques</u>, I:39, 96; II: 166; VI:4, 118.

1931   J. Sturm, <u>Archiv für Orientforschung</u> 7, 187-192.

1937   A. Jirku, <u>Die ägyptischen Listen palästinensischer und syrischen Ortsnamen</u>, <u>Klio</u> Beiheft 38.

1937   J. Simons, <u>Handbook for the Study of Egyptian Topographical Lists</u>. See Index.

1939   S.A.B. Mercer, <u>The Tell el-Amarna Tablets</u>.

1939   G. Dossin, <u>Syria</u> 20, 111f.

1940   G. Hill, <u>A History of Cyprus</u>.

1945   J. Vergote, <u>Phonétique historique de l'égyptien</u>, 135f

1947   C.H. Gordon, "The new Amarna Tablets", <u>Orientalia</u> 16.

1949   J. Yoyotte, "Les stèles de Ramses II a Tanis", <u>Kêmi</u> 10, p. 73, note 3.

1950   A. Jirku, "The Problem of Alashiya", <u>PEQ</u> 82, 40-42.

1952   O. Gurney, <u>The Hittites</u>.

1952   C.F.A. Schaeffer, <u>Enkomi-Alasia, 1946-1950</u>.

1953   D. Wiseman, <u>The Alalakh Tablets</u> 8f.

1953   O. Eissfeldt, "Ugarit und Alaschia", <u>DLZ</u> 74, 249-252.

1954   R. Caminos, <u>Late-Egyptian Miscellanies</u>, 200f, 209f.

1956   J. Vercoutter, <u>L'Egypte et le monde égéen préhéllenique</u>, pp. 89, 97, 166, 181, note 4.

1961   O. Masson, "Les inscriptions chypriotes syllabiques", <u>Etudes Chypriotes</u>, 228f.

1962   W. Helck, <u>Die Beziehungen Ägyptens zu Vorderasien</u> 289f, 404f, 416f.

1962   G. Steiner, "Neue Alašiya-texte", <u>Kadmos</u> I, 130-138.

1963   A. Herdner, "Corpus des tablettes en cunéiforme alpha betiques" <u>Mission de Ras Shamra</u> 10.

1964   E. Hornung, Untersuchungen zur Chronologie und Geschichte des Neuen Reiches, 108f

1964   H. Catling, Cypriote Bronzework in the Mycenaean World 299f

1965   C.H. Gordon, Ugaritic Textbook.

1966   P. Åstrom, Excavations at Kalopsidha etc. (SMA 11), 139f.

1966   E. Edel, Die Ortsnamenlisten aus dem Totentempel Amenophis III, 71f, 83f, 76f

1966   H. W. Catling, "Cyprus in the Neolithic and Bronze Age Periods", Cambridge Ancient History, II, chapter XXII (b).

1967   R.S. Merrillees, Review of P. Åstrom, Excavations at Kalopsidha, in Antiquity 41, 333f.

1967   H. G. Güterbock, "The Hittite Conquest of Cyprus Reconsidered", JNES 26, 73-81.

1967   M. Kanawaty, Toutankhamon et son temps, 50f

1967   G. Bass, Cape Gelidonya: A Bronze Age Shipwreck, The American Philosophical Society, Philadelphia, 77f

1968   R. S. Merrillees, The Cypriote Bronze Age Pottery Found in Egypt, (SMA 18), pp. viii f.

1968   M. J. Mellink, Review of H.W. Catling's chapter inCAH, JAOS 88, 539f.

1969   H. Otten, Sprachliche Stellung und Datierung des Madduwatta Textes, 33f.

1970   A. F. Rainey, El-Amarna Tablets 359-379.

1971   Y. Lynn Holmes, "The Location of Alashiya", JAOS 91, 426-429.

1971   C. F-A. Schaeffer, Alasia, 20th campaign of excavation at Enkomi/Alasia (sic).

1971   A. Caquot and R. du Mesnil du Buisson, Syria 48, 391-406.

1972   P. Åstrom, The Late Cypriote Bronze Age, Historical Conclusions, Part I, The Swedish Cyprus Expedition, 772, 778f.

224

1972   R. S. Merrillees, "Alashiya", <u>Praktika tou protou</u> <u>Kyprologikou Synedriou I</u>, Nicosia, 111-119.

1972   J. D. Muhly, "The Land of Alashiya", the same volume, 201-219.

1973   O. Masson, "A propos de l'île d'Alasia", <u>Kadmos</u> 12, 98f.

1977   E. Lipinski, "An Ugaritic Letter to Amenophis III Concerning Trade with Alashiya", <u>Iraq</u> 39, 213-217.

1978   J. Leclant, "Le nom de Chypre dans les textes hiéroglyphiques", Colloques Internationaux du C.N.R.S. no. 578, <u>Salamine de Chypre</u>, 131-135.

1979   H. Georgiou, "Relations between Cyprus and the Near East in the Middle and Late Bronze Age", <u>Levant</u> XI, 84-100.

1979   L. Hellbing, <u>Alasia Problems</u> (<u>SMA</u> 57).

1980   J. Strange, <u>Caphthor/Keftiu</u>, 168-184.

1982   J.D. Muhly and others, <u>Early Metallurgy in Cyprus</u>.

1982   Y. Lynn Holmes, "The Isy-Ars Controversy", <u>Studia</u> <u>Hierosolymitana</u>, ed. S. Groll, 317-334.

1983   W. Helck, "Asija", <u>ZAS</u> 110, 29-36.

1985   A. Nibbi, <u>Wenamun and Alashiya Reconsidered</u>.

IRS/ALASA/ALASHIYA

Footnotes

1. H. Gauthier, Dictionnaire des noms géographiques (1925), I: 39, 96; II: 166; VI: 4, 118.

2. J.A. Knudtzon, Die El-Amarna-Tafeln (1915), 296-7. See also English translation by S.A.B. Mercer (1939).

3. A. Erman, ZAS 27 (1889), 63. This forms part of Winckler's study and we must bear in mind the fact the numbering of the Letters is prior to Knudtzon's.

4. W. Fischer, "Der Beitrag der Araber zur Ortsnamengebung im Vorderen Orient", Erlanger Ortsnamen Colloquium 1980, Beiträge zur Namenforschung Beiheft 18, pp. 27-31.

5. ibid. 30f

6. O. Bates, The Eastern Libyans (1914), 79ff.

7. Zeitschrift für Assyriologie X, 262f.

8. KRI I, 33 no. 12 and 34 no.36.

9. KRI II, 620.

10. J. Simons, Handbook for the Study of Egyptian Topographical Lists Relating to Western Asia (1937), see Index. See also E. Edel, "Die Ortsnamen in den Tempeln von Aksha, Amarah und Soleb im Sudan", Biblische Notizen 11 (1980). Also by Edel, "Die Ortsnamenlisten aus dem Totentempel Amenophis III", Bonner Biblische Beiträge 25 (1966).

11. G. A. Wainwright in Klio 14, 1-36; Lynn Holmes in S. Groll, ed. Studia Hierosolymitana (1982), 317-334; W. Helck, ZAS 110 (1983) 29-36.

12. Die Statistische Tafel von Karnak 47f.

13. "The land of Alashiya", Journal of the Manchester Oriental Society, 36f.

14. "Alasia", Praktika tou protou Kyprologikou Synedriou I Nicosia 1972, p. 116, note 7.

15. Klio 14, 1-36.

16. ibid. 17f.

17. see note 11 above.

18. ibid.

19. _Recueil de Travaux_ 10, 209f.

20. _Voyage d'un égyptien_ (1866), 225f.

21. _PSBA_ 10, 488-525.

22. ibid. 540-569 and Plates VIII and IX.

23. _Asien und Europa_.

24. ibid. 261f.

25. Max Müller, 1893 cit., 394f.

26. ibid. 395.

27. Max Müller 1895, cit. note 7 above.

28. ibid. 264f.

29. We now know that copper was available from many
     sources on the Near Eastern mainland, as well as on
     the Greek mainland. We also know that it was
     plentiful in the southern Sinai, as we shall see
     in our detailed discussion below.

30. _Klio_ 14 (1915), 1-36.

31. _JEA_ 64 (1978), 56-64. Apart from the sign's
     representation of the pack-saddle, we must remember
     that stt was the name of the southern Nile island of
     Sehel. This may have been a gathering place for the
     trade caravans travelling south to north and vice
     versa.

32. ibid. p. 62.

33. 3f. _Urk. IV_, 893.

34. _AESEN_, 158,163

35. Wainwright cit. 5ff

36. ibid. 6f

37. ibid. 7f

38. ibid. 8

39. ibid. 8f

40. ibid. 9f

41. ibid. 27f

42. ibid.

43. Mariette, Karnak Plates 28-31; PM II, 120-1.

44. AESEN, Plate 22. See also Urk. IV 24f and note p.25. This contradicts the statement of R.D. Barnett in his chapter on "The Sea Peoples", CAH, Vol. II, Chapter 28, p. 16 of Fasc. 68. He suggests these animals were used only in Anatolia.

45. SPE p. 111. These animals which we know were in use in the quarries near Cairo early in the Eighteenth Dynasty are shown again during the reign of Ramesses III, pulling the carts of foreign peoples.

46. Wainwright, cit. 27f.

47. See our long chapter on Wenamun.

48. Klio 17 (1921), 230-239.

49. Section I, 39 and 96; Section II, 166; Section VI, 4, 118.

50. Section I, 96.

51. "Les stèles de Ramses II a Tanis", Kêmi 10, 73 note 3.

52. L'Egypte et le monde égéen préhéllenique.

53. Die Beziehungen Ägyptens zu Vorderasien see Index.

54. "The Problem of Alashiya", PEQ 82, 40-42.

55. "Neue Alašija-texte", pp. 130-138.

56. Pritchard, ANET (1955), 119ff, 201ff.

57. cit. 136.

58. Kadmos 12 (1973), 98f.

59. "The Hittite Conquest of Cyprus Reconsidered", JNES 26, 73-81.

60. ibid. 80f.

61. 74ff and 80f.

62. Vol. II, Chapter XXII (b), section IX.

63.   ibid.

64.   ibid.

65.   JAOS 88, 540f.

66.   Sprachliche Stellung und Datierung des Madduwatta-
      Textes (1969), 33f.

67.   JAOS 91, 426-429.

68.   ibid. 429f.

69.   ibid. 427f.

70.   ibid.

71.   "The Isj-Ars Controversy", Studia Hierosolymitana,
      ed. S. Groll, 317-334.

72.   ibid. 322f.

73.   Praktika tou protou Kyprologikou Synedriou I,
      Nicosia, 1972.

74.   ibid. 111-119.

75.   ibid. 114f.

76.   See note 10 above.

77.   118f.

78.   ibid.

79.   ibid. 201-219.

80.   ibid. 201f

81.   204ff. 208f.

82.   ibid. 202.

83.   ibid. 203f. Most of these points had been made by
      Wainwright in 1915.

84.   ibid. 202f.

85.   ibid. 203.

86.   ibid. 204f.

87.   ibid.

88. ibid. 204f.

89. ibid. 205.

90. ibid. 207f.

91. ibid. 205ff.

92. 207f.

93. ibid.

94. 208f

95. This was noted also by Merrillees and others.

96. Section iii) below.

97. cit. 208.

98. ibid. 213ff.

99. ibid. 209ff.

100. None of the proper names on these lists have been studied in much depth and our understanding of them is hypothetical only.

101. We must remember that he also began his discussion by accepting this hypothesis.

102. "Relations between Cyprus and the Near East in the Middle and Late Bronze Age", Levant 11 (1979), 84-100.

103. ibid. 84f.

104. see note 66 above.

105. cit. 87ff.

106. ibid. 88f and 92f

107. ibid. 90f

108. Alasia Problems. Studies in Mediterrranean Archaeology, 57 (1979).

109. Caphthor/Keftiu: A New Investigation, particularly 168-184.

110. ibid. 182-184.

111. Salamine de Chypre: Histoire et Archéologie, Colloques Internationaux du C.N.R.S. No. 578, 131-135.

112.   ibid. 133f.

113.   We are therefore prompted to ask whether this town
        can originally have been part of the greater region
        of Alashiya. It does seem to extend this region very
        far to the west.

114.   In spite of the surveys by Beno Rothenberg in
        recent years and others in earlier years,
        specific and properly published information about
        this area is not yet available to us.

115.   Israel Exploration Journal 23 (1973), 198-205.

116.   ibid. 198f, 200f.

117.   ibid. 200, note 7.

118.   ibid. 202f.

119.   ibid. 204.

120.   Levant 15 (1983), 39-48.

121.   Levant 17 (1985), 89-116.

122.   cit. pp. 32-36.

123.   Studia Hierosolymitana ed. S. Groll, 1982, 317-334.

124.   Holmes questions the authenticity of the Egyptian
        document in this case and not our understanding of
        it.

125.   There are a great many names on the Egyptian lists
        which we can not identify.

126.   Nibbi, The Sea Peoples: A Re-Examination of the
        Egyptian Sources. This was followed in 1975 by
        The Sea Peoples and Egypt (Noyes Press, New Jersey).

127.   LEM, p. 209.

128.   AESEN, Plate 22.

129.   As we referred to earlier, from the lists in the
        Papyrus Harris.

130.   URK. IV, 650, line 35.

131.   Shown on A. R. Guest's map of Lower Egypt showing
        the principal canals of the Nile and the
        Kurahs or administrative divisions in the 10th and
        12th centuries A.D.

132. A study of the oils mentioned in the Papyrus Anastasi IV was made recently by Manfred Görg, "Öle aus dem Ausland", SAK 11 (1984), 219-226. Earlier we had H. Altenmüller, "Das Ölmagazin im Grab des Hesire in Saqqara", SAK 4 (1976), 1-29. We now also have the study of plants in ancient Egypt by R. Germer, Untersuchung uber Arzneimittelpflanzen im Alten Ägypten (1979). More recently she has published Flora des Pharaonischen Ägypten (1985), bringing together the work of Vivi Täckholm and other botanists who had worked in earlier years.

133. Nibbi, JARCE XIV (1977), 59.

134. We know the ingots are seen on the Egyptian reliefs in brick, bun, and oxhide shape. See Nibbi, "Some Remarks on Copper", JARCE XIV (1977), 59-66. See our fig. 13 here. Caminos, LEM 218f. Also in ring shapes.

135. This mistake is recently made in an article on copper by Claire Lalouette, whose interest is clearly literary rather than practical: "Le 'Firmament de Cuivre' ", in BIFAO 79 (1979), 333-353. An earlier discussion on copper may be found in R. Drenkhahn's chapter on Metallbearbeitung, 1976.

136. Nibbi, op. cit. 60f.

137. BAR IV, p. 193

138. ibid. p. 160, third line on page.

139. J. R. Harris, Lexicographical Studies in Ancient Egyptian Minerals (1961); see also now the Lexikon für Ägyptologie ed. Helck and Otto.

140. N. de Garis Davies, The Tomb of Rekh-Mi-Re at Thebes I and II, (1943).

141. op. cit.

142. Caminos LEM, 218f.

143. Erichsen, Papyrus Harris I p. 25

144. "The Composition of Copper Alloys used by the Greek, Etruscan and Roman Civilisations", Journal of Archaeological Science 3 (1976), 93-113; ibid. 4 (1977), 103-123, see particularly here 107f.

145. cit. LEM 218f.

146. J. A. Knudtzon, Die El-Amarna Tafeln (1915); S. A. B.
      Mercer, The Tell El-Amarna Tablets (1939); A. F.
      Rainey, El-Amarna Tablets 359-379, (1970).

147. The title of his work published in 1979 refers to the
      problems concerning Alasia.

148. Ancient Byblos Reconsidered (1985), 5f, 38f;
      hereafter ABR.

149. ibid. 72-78

150. ibid. 25ff, 59ff.

151. Hellbing, cit. 90f.

152. AESEN chapter 1; ABR, 15-25.

153. Mariner's Mirror 65 (1979), 201-208; ibid. 70 (1984),
      247-266.

154. cit. 41f.

155. Syria 20 (1939), 111f.

156. J.D. Muhly cit. 1972, 204f.

157. Texts AT 385 and AT 269, Muhly cit. p. 205.

158. C.H. Gordon, Ugaritic Textbook (1965); A. Herdner,
      Corpus des tablettes etc. (1963), cit.

159. cit. p. 206.

160. cit. p. 207.

161. H. Otten, Sprachliche Stellung und Datierung des
      Madduwatta-Textes (1969), 33f.

162. Scholars have disputed the meaning of these
      passages and we shall not attempt to enter into this
      discussion here.

163. See Güterbock, JNES 26 (1967), 73-81.

164. We know that the Near Eastern city was of this size,
      as were also many ancient Greek cities. We now know
      more about the administration of the ancient Near
      Eastern city since the Ebla archives came to
      light. See G. Pettinato and P. Matthiae, "Aspetti
      amministrativi topografici di Ebla nel III
      millennio av. Cr. ", Rivista degli Studi Orientali
      (1976), 1-30.

165. cit. 89f.

166. <u>The Sea Peoples: Warriors of the Ancient Mediterranean</u>
(1978), 18f.

167. It is absolutely useless to us all to re-assert the
traditional view of the Sea Peoples so-called
without attempting to understand the underlying
problems which prevent us from seeing a true
picture of these events. Furthermore, many
distinguished scholars have been totally
undisturbed by the consideration of all kinds of
so-called evidence, without properly addressing the
Egyptian texts which are the only sources for
the assumption that the attackers of Egypt came
<u>from the sea</u>.

168. It is now being accepted by Egyptologists that
neither <u>Great Green</u> nor <u>ym</u> can be shown to mean
<u>sea</u> at any time.

169. The whole problem of <u>Alasia</u> has risen from the
erroneous interpretation of the story of Wenamun
which has him sailing on the Mediterranean (sic)
in search of cedar (sic) so that when he is blown
off course, the nearest land is Cyprus. Had this
story been interpreted more literally, and
therefore more accurately, the problem of
Alasa/Alashiya and its whereabouts would never have
arisen, because this place would soon have been
identified on the north shore of Lake Timsah.

170. Our site for Alashiya seems to be suitable for
isolating prisoners because it was in the middle of
a swampland infested with crocodiles.

171. The site of the present town of Ismailia, part of
which is still called Arasha/Arashiya today, may
well have been an island in earlier times
before the swampland was drained.

172. <u>Kadmos</u> 12 (1973), 98f.

173. <u>Syria</u> 48, 391-406.

174. This was of course compared to other finds from
Cyprus itself, see Wainwright, cit. 5ff,
indicating the title <u>from Alashiya</u>, but this does not
necessarily indicate a Cypriote provenance.

175. Plate 31 of the geographical volume of plates.

176. So far we have only partial surveys of the vast
area. In their study of this area in Volume I of the

234

Annals of the Geological Survey of Egypt (November, 1971), S. El Akkad and A.M. Abdullah list the work of their predecessors in this field, Blankenhorn (1901 and 1921), Cuvillier (1930), Sadek (1926), Zaatout (1956), Said (1962), Selim (1965).

177.   Soc. d'études de l'Isthme de Suez, Vol. 2, 21-4. He was surprised to find the gyps fulva eagle on this mountain in 1948.

178.   "Les monts d'Attaka", Bull. Soc. de Geog. Vol. 20, 1939-42.

179.   cit. 21f

180.   ibid.

181.   ibid. 22f.

182.   E. Erichsen, The Papyrus Harris I, from Plate 75 onwards.

183.   Plate 78, lines 1ff. Also Breasted Ancient Records of Egypt Vol. IV, par. 468.

184.   Breasted's translation was always careful so that we may at present find no better translation of this passage than his.

185.   On the problems concerning Punt see AESEN chapters 5 and 6.

186.   I published a series of small articles on this theme in Göttinger Miszellen from 1975 onwards, including a warning of the fast development along this area which destroyed its banks totally within a short space of time.

187.   This dates from the Napoleonic period and one may assume that the name has continued to be used from earlier times.

188.   Kadmos I, 130ff.

189.   cit. 204f.

190.   Steiner, cit. Kadmos I (1962), 131f.

191.   A. Bernard Knapp, JCS 32 (1980), 43-47.

192.   ibid. 44f

193.   A.R. Millard, JCS 25 (1973), 211-213.

194. <u>AESEN</u>, chapters 5 and 6.

195. Scholars must take <u>all</u> the evidence into account, including the fish frieze (<u>AESEN</u>, chapter 4) before indicating a location for Punt.

196. E. Oren, cit. <u>IEJ</u> 23 (1973), 198-205.

197. ibid. 202f.

198. Introduction to <u>The Inscriptions of Sinai</u> (1952-5).

199. <u>Levant</u> 15 (1983), 39-48; <u>Levant</u> 17 (1985), 89-116; also B. Rothenberg, "Sinai Explorations", <u>Museum Haaretz Bulletin</u> 1967-1972; also <u>PEQ</u>, 1970, 1-29.

200. A. H. Gardiner, T. E. Peet and J. Černý, <u>The Inscriptions of Sinai</u> (1952-5).

201. B. Rothenberg, <u>Timna</u> (1972).

202. See note 199 above.

203. J. Couyat and P. Montet, <u>Les inscriptions hiéroglyphiques et hiératiques du Ouadi Hammamat</u>, MIFAO 34 (1912). Also G. Goyon, <u>Nouvelles inscriptions rupestres du Ouadi Hammamat</u> (1957).

204. A. Nibbi, "Some Remarks on the Two Stelae from the Wadi Gasus", <u>JEA</u> 62 (1976), 45-46.

205. G. A Moustafa and M. E. Hilmy, <u>Geological Survey and Mineral Research Department</u>, Paper no. 5 (1958); see also Paper no. 12 (1962) by G. A Moustafa and M. Kamal Akkad.

206. G. Vantini, <u>Oriental Sources Concerning Nubia</u> (1975), pp. 653, 727, 729.

207. ibid. 111f

208. "Chemical and lead isotope analysis of ancient Egyptian gold, silver and lead" in <u>Archaeo Physika</u> 10 (1979), 299-314 as well as studies of silver in the Agean context, references to which are made in their article of 1981, cit.

209. "Silver in Ancient Times", <u>JEA</u> 14, 313-319. 210. Vantini, cit. 277f

211. ibid. 112f

212. ibid. 151f.

213.   ibid. 244f

214.   ibid. 126f

215.   ibid. 99f

216.   ibid. 100f

217.   op. cit. 11f

218.   ibid. 71f

219.   "Alasiya of the Amarna Letters", JNES 35 (1976).

220.   op. cit. p. V.

221.   1983, pp. 489-492.

222.   J. C. Payne, "Lapis Lazuli in early Egypt", Iraq 30 (1968) 58-61.

223.   G. Herrmann, "Lapis Lazuli: the early phases of its trade", Iraq 30 (1968), 12-57.

224.   AESEN 45f; GM nos. 19 and 22 (1976).

225.   op. cit. p. 490

226.   "The Stt Sign", JEA 64 (1978).

227.   G. Vantini, Oriental Sources Concerning Nubia (1975), 280f

228.   The Travels and Adventures of Edward Brown Esq. London, 1739, p. 312

229.   See Belegestellen, Vol. III, p. 99.

230.   Faulkner, Coffin Texts, Vol. II, 192.

231.   Witzel, Hethitische Keilschrift Urk. (1924), Vol. IV, 80f.

List of Figures

1. Map showing the position of Rhakotis, identified by the so-called Pompey's Pillar. It is important to understand that this ancient, native settlement was situated, <u>not</u> on the Mediterranean Sea, but on the north shore of Lake Mareotis.

2. (a) Map showing the whole course of the Wadi Tumilat, which carried the Nile water eastwards and flowed into Lake Timsah, then southwards. El Gibali which I am suggesting was the kbn/kpnj of the Egyptian texts, lies on the south-western shore of Lake Timsah, though it is largely destroyed today.

   (b) Detail of the area near Lake Timsah, into which the Wadi Tumilat flowed.

3. The southernmost limits of Syria and Phoenicia as seen by the Graeco-Romans, after Murray's <u>Classical Atlas,</u> Plate 1.

4. The Near Eastern coast showing the places to which we refer in this study.

5. Map showing the towns from the root of <u>jrs</u>, including the very extensive Wadi El Arish, the name of which we believe to be derived from this same root. The area inhabited by the El ^CArayish Beduin in the northern Sinai is also shown, as well as the two towns called El ^CAras, one of them west of Bilbeis.

6. Here we see the water channels taking the Nile water along the natural depression eastwards into the Wadi Tumilat.

7. Detail of the area called Sahhara today and also El Gibali, along the western shore of Lake Timsah.

8. A suggestion for the route of Wenamun's journey.

9. A detail of the position of Gebel Attaqah, possibly the Taggata of the Hittite texts.

10. The writing of Irs/Alasa in the Egyptian texts.

11. Some settlement patterns in the northern Sinai, after Oren.

12. (a) Kheta people as depicted with usual shields in the Egyptian reliefs and (b) Hittites with their usual shields as depicted in Anatolia. To judge from this iconography only, there is no similarity between them.

13. This sketch shows (a) a vessel for melting the copper and (b), (c) and (d) indisputable ingot shapes.

14. Quotation from the Papyrus Harris, Plate 21 b, line 14, after Erichsen.

15. Quotation from Papyrus Anastasi IV, 17: 7-8, after Gardiner.

16. The area which we are suggesting was probably the ancient region of Alasa/Alashiya is shown cross-hatched in this sketch map.

17. Sketch map showing the important copper and gold-bearing sites in the Eastern desert and the Sinai, as well as sites which have produced galena and tin.

18. These figures are shown to be carrying two shapes of ingot.
    (a) In the earlier scene, they are carrying brick shapes. This block, unfortunately of unknown provenance, dates from the Old Kingdom and is now in the Cairo Museum (W. M. Müller, Egyptological Researches I, Plate 1). These figures are stated to be carrying lead ingots and each ingot appears to have a hole at its forward end perhaps to allow it to be carried hanging from the pack-saddle of a donkey. Thus it is clear that lead ingots were used during the Old Kingdom, just as the Papyrus Anastasi IV tells us was the case in the New Kingdom, carried by the children of Alasa.

    (b) The portrayal of ox-hide shaped ingots here is from the tomb of Rekhmire (New Kingdom), see Norman de Garis Davis, Paintings from the Tomb of Rekhmire, Plates 3, 5 and 12. The ox-hide shaped ingot first appears in the Egyptian iconography in the Middle Kingdom (see Nibbi, Discussions in Egyptology 4, 1986, forthcoming).

List of abbreviations of publications which
may not be found in the usual lists of journals.

ABR   A. Nibbi, Ancient Byblos Reconsidered (1985).

AE   W. Max Müller, Asien und Europa (1893).

AEO   A.H. Gardiner, Ancient Egyptian Onomastica (1947).

AESEN   A. Nibbi, Ancient Egypt and Some Eastern Neighbours
        (1981).

BAR   J. Breasted, Ancient Records of Egypt (1906).

DE   Discussion in Egyptology (1985-).

IFAO   Institut français d'archéologie orientale (Le Caire).

KRI   K.A. Kitchen, Ramesside Inscriptions (1968-).

LD   R. Lepsius, Denkmäler Ägypten und Äthiopien
        1897-1913.

LES   A.H. Gardiner, Late Egyptian Stories (1932).

GM   Göttinger Miszellen (1972-).

Goedicke   H. Goedicke, The Report of Wenamun (1975).

LEM Caminos   R. Caminos, Late-Egyptian Miscellanies (1954).

LEM Gardiner A.H. Gardiner, Late-Egyptian Miscellanies
             (1937).

Lexikon   W. Helck and H. Otto, Lexikon für Ägyptologie
           (1975-).

Lichtheim I   M. Lichtheim, Ancient Egyptian Literature I,
              The Old and Middle Kingdoms (1973).

Lichtheim II M. Lichtheim, Ancient Egyptian Literature II,
              The New Kingdom (1976).

PM   B. Porter and R. Moss, ed. J. Málek, Topographical
        Bibliography of Ancient Egyptian Hieroglyphic Texts,
        Reliefs and Paintings (1927-51). Second edition now
        in progress.

SPE   A. Nibbi, The Sea Peoples and Egypt (1975).

Urk. I K. Sethe, Urkunden des alten Reiches (1903).

Urk. IV K. Sethe, Urkunden der 18. Dynastie (1927-30).

Printed for DE Publications, 13 Lovelace Rd., Oxford,
OX2 8LP, by Bocardo Press, Cowley, Oxford OX4 2EY.